The Fundamentals
WATERCOLOUR
LANDSCAPES
Paintings for all seasons

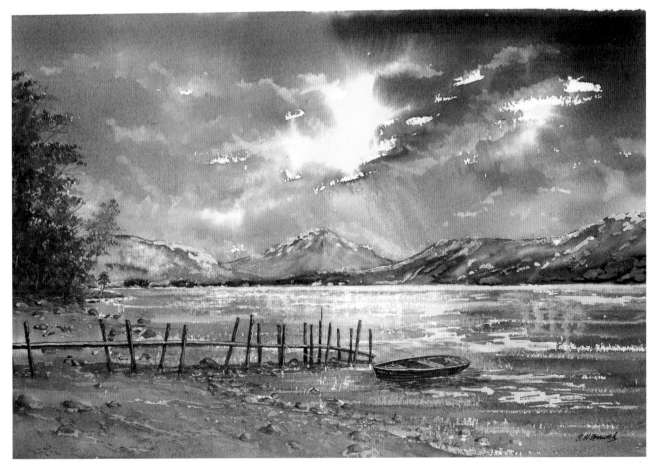

Keith Fenwick

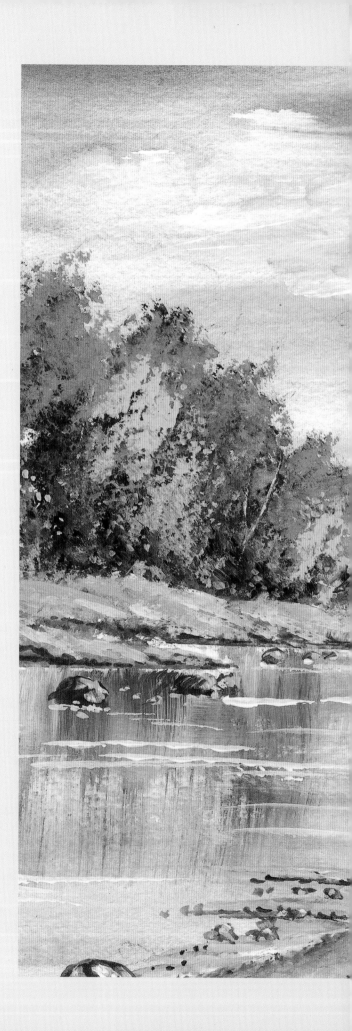

ARCTURUS

This edition published in 2014 by Arcturus Publishing Limited
26/27 Bickels Yard, 151–153 Bermondsey Street,
London SE1 3HA

Copyright © Arcturus Holdings Limited

ISBN: 978-1-78404-222-6
AD004236UK

Printed in China

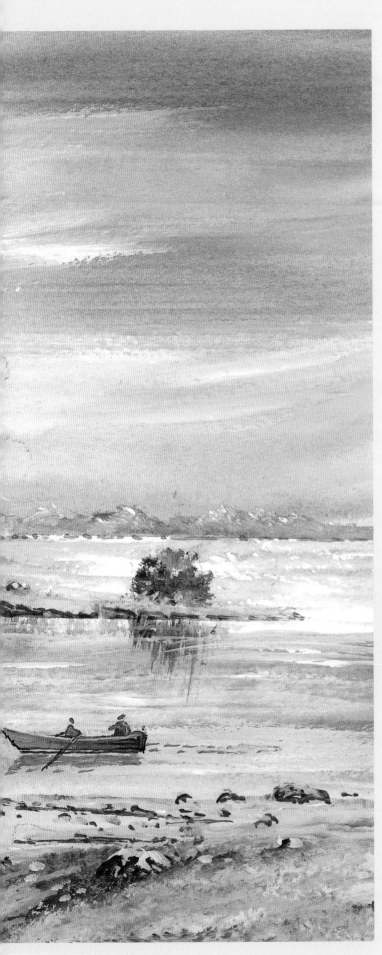

CONTENTS

INTRODUCTION   5

MATERIALS AND EQUIPMENT   6

WATERCOLOUR TECHNIQUES   8

DESIGN PRINCIPLES   12

THE IMPORTANCE OF TONAL STUDIES   16

SPRING   21

PROJECTS/CLOSE UPS   **22–41, 46–53, 56–57, 68–73**

COMPOSITION   42

PAINTING SKIES   54

COLOUR MIXING   58

PAINTING WATER   66

PAINTING MOUNTAINS AND ROCKS   74

SUMMER   77

PROJECTS/CLOSE UPS   **78–85, 88–95**

PERSPECTIVE MADE SIMPLE   86

HOW TO PAINT TREES   96

AUTUMN   101

PROJECTS/CLOSE UPS   **102–111**

WINTER   113

PROJECTS/CLOSE UPS   **114–125**

THE WAY FORWARD   126

PORTRAIT OF THE ARTIST   128

SPRING

Leaves that are bursting open
Daffodil buds uncurled
This is the giving of glory
The offer of gold to the world

SUMMER

And all the goodness of the earth
Shall shine in glad array
As if lifetime's loveliness
Lived in one summer's day

AUTUMN

A world of wealth and wonders
Where the leaves dance as they fall
And all we lack is just the time
To go and see it all

WINTER

A fairyland of wisdom
In the filigree of frost
Where the golden leaves have fallen
And the foliage is lost.

Kathleen Partridge

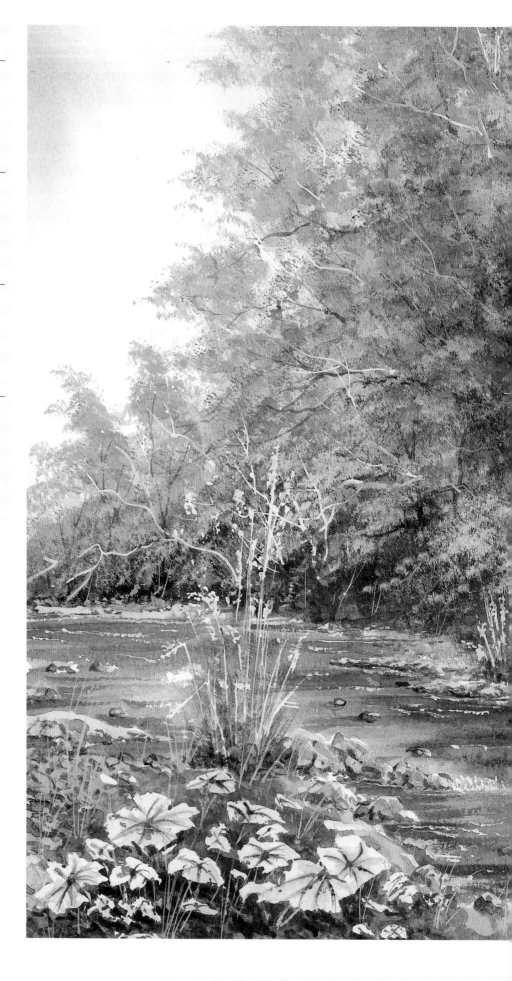

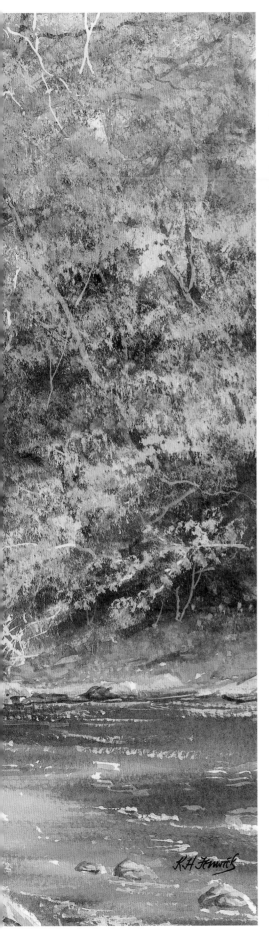

INTRODUCTION

The landscapes in this book represent the artist's year, from the gradual awakening of life in spring to the blossoming of colour through summer and autumn and the gradual slowing down of nature in the cold of winter.

My aim in this book is to show my approach to painting a landscape from concept to finished picture, in the hope that the techniques I describe will be of use to both the beginner and the more experienced painter.

I have never believed that being able to paint is a gift; whatever you wish to achieve in life has to be worked for. Watercolour painting is no exception, but it is easier than you may think and by means of this book, I hope to prove it to you. Running workshops and painting holidays over many years has verified my belief that anyone can be taught to paint. All I ask of you is that you practise the techniques I am going to show you and follow the logical process I describe. By following these techniques and applying the principles of design you will soon be able to produce paintings that will give you immense satisfaction and pleasure. Don't forget, 'practice makes perfect' – winners never quit and quitters never win.

Painting is a wonderful pastime – it will change your life. Just ask any artist! You will see things you have never noticed before and appreciate more fully the wonders of nature.

It is an artist's dream to see their paintings in book form and to know from the many phone calls and letters received that in a small way they are helping other artists to fulfil their dreams and aspirations. In my paintings, I attempt to capture the ever-changing light and mood in the landscape. What better way to present them to you than by painting the seasons of the year?

Happy painting!
Keith Fenwick

HOW TO USE THIS BOOK

If you are a novice, begin by studying the sections dealing with the basic materials, the principles of design, colour mixing, techniques for painting the elements and, most importantly, the section covering tonal values. Follow this by attempting the more simple projects, then as your skills and confidence grow you can tackle more advanced subjects.

A more experienced painter may still have difficulties painting certain elements such as skies, trees, and so on. I suggest you work through the projects and close-ups, referring to the sections dealing with the elements with which you are having problems. To give yourself an extra challenge, try painting projects in a different season to the ones portrayed.

MATERIALS & EQUIPMENT

There is a school of thought that says beginners may as well purchase brushes, paper and paints from the cheaper ranges when starting out. Having run workshops and painting holidays for many years and observed at first hand the difficulties that beginners encounter using such materials, I don't share this opinion. I recommend you purchase the best materials you can afford – your investment will work out cheaper in the long term and your frustration will be considerably less.

PAINTS

Whether you use pans of paint or tube colours is a matter of choice. Most professional artists prefer tube colours because they are more convenient for mixing large washes and are moist and more easily used for general painting. Pans of paint become very hard and release less colour if left unused. They are more suitable for carrying on holiday and for sketching purposes.

The choice of colours is personal to the artist, but you won't go far wrong if you begin with my basic palette. As you progress, you can purchase additional colours as required.

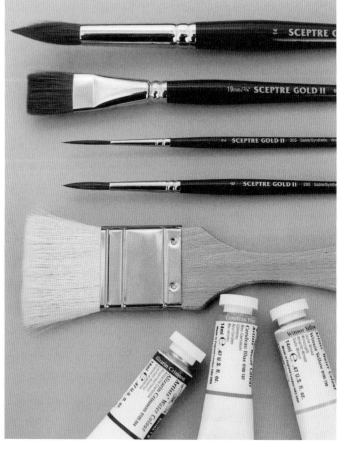

BASIC PALETTE

SKY	EARTH	MIXERS
Payne's Grey	Raw Sienna	Cadmium Yellow Pale
Cerulean	Burnt Sienna	Permanent Sap Green
Alizarin Crimson	Burnt Umber	

SUPPORTIVE PALETTE

French Ultramarine	Gold Ochre	Brown Madder
Cobalt Blue	Winsor Yellow	Vermilion
	Winsor Red	Purple Madder

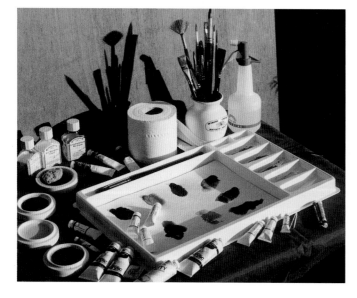

BRUSHES

For painting skies and other large areas, I use a 38 mm/1½ in hake brush. For control, I use a size 14 round, for buildings and angular shapes, a 19 mm/¾ in flat brush and for detail, a size 3 or larger rigger brush. A size 6 round brush is useful for shadows and when painting smaller elements.

PALETTE

I prefer to use a palette that has a large open area for colour mixing, allowing me to draw my colours into the centre and mix them to my requirements. For larger washes, I pre-mix them in ceramic saucers. One of the greatest difficulties my students experience is attempting to mix colours on palettes with small indentations to hold paint and a very limited mixing area. Don't give yourself unnecessary problems; purchase a large palette.

PAPERS

Paper can be purchased in gummed pads, spiral-bound pads, blocks (where the paper is glued all round, except for a small area where the sheets can be separated) and in sheet form. The sheets are less expensive and can be cut to the required size.

Good-quality paper is available in various textures and weights. The paintings in this book were executed mainly on 425 gsm/ 200 lb and 640 gsm/300 lb rough-textured paper, with a few on the thinner 300 gsm/140 lb. This last needs stretching if heavy washes are to be applied in order to avoid it cockling (developing an uneven surface). This is done by soaking the paper and then securing it to a drawing board using gummed brown paper (not masking tape) all round the edge. As the paper dries it shrinks, held flat by the gummed paper. I prefer the two heavier papers, which don't need stretching. In fact, I have never stretched paper in 20 years, although many artists do.

There are three basic surfaces:
HP (Hot pressed) has a smooth surface, suitable for calligraphy and pen and wash.

NOT (Cold pressed, or CP) has a slight texture (called the 'tooth') and is used by the majority of artists.

ROUGH or EXTRA ROUGH paper has a more pronounced texture, which I prefer. It is wonderful for skies, tree foliage, dry-brush techniques and creating sparkle on water.

ACCESSORIES

The following items, most of which can be seen in the lower photograph opposite, complete my painting kit:

Toilet roll or tissues: for creating skies, applying textures and cleaning palettes.

Mediums: art masking fluid, permanent masking medium, granulation medium and lifting preparation are all selectively used in my paintings.

Masking tape: this is used to control the flow of paint, mask areas in the painting and fasten paper to the backing board. I prefer the 19 mm/¾ in width as it is easier to remove.

Cocktail sticks: useful for applying masking when fine lines are required.

Greaseproof paper: for masking.

Atomizer bottle: for spraying paper with clean water or paint.

Painting board: your board should be 5 cm/2 in larger all round than the size of your watercolour painting. Always secure your paper at each corner and each side (eight places) to prevent it from cockling when you are painting.

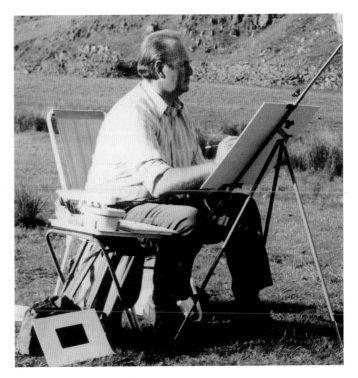

Eraser: a putty eraser is ideal for removing masking.

Sponge: natural sponges are useful for removing colour and creating tree foliage, texture on rocks and so on.

Water-soluble crayons: for drawing outlines, correcting mistakes and adding highlights.

Palette knife: for moving paint around on the paper (see page 75).

Saucers: for mixing large washes and pouring paint.

Hairdryer: for drying paint between stages.

Easel and stool: I occasionally use a lightweight easel and a stool for outdoor work.

PAINTING OUTDOORS

I like to be comfortable when painting outdoors. The photograph above shows the set-up I prefer. If I am painting a scene that isn't too far from the car I carry a folding chair, but where I have to walk a considerable distance, I usually sit on a rock or wall. A lightweight metal easel is useful for holding the paper/board. For carrying materials to my destination, I have a haversack that is combined with a stool. The latter then acts as a support for my palette and water pot. As the photograph shows, this set-up provides a very convenient painting station. The viewfinder, here propped against the haversack, helps me to choose the best composition.

WATERCOLOUR TECHNIQUES

Watercolourists have a wide range of techniques available to them to use in their paintings, some very common, some more imaginative. The more experienced watercolourist will know which basic technique to use to paint a particular element in their painting and which special technique to employ for a specific texture or effect. In the following pages, I have shown a wide range of techniques for you to practise. Some will be used in every painting, while others will only be selected as needed to create a special effect.

FLAT WASH
This is created by brushing a fluid paint evenly over a damp or dry surface.

GRADED WASH
As the flat wash, but add more water to each brush stroke as you work down.

VARIEGATED WASH
As the flat wash but change the colours between brush strokes.

GLAZING
Useful effects can be achieved by brushing various washes over a dry underpainting.

DRY BRUSH
A paint-loaded damp brush washed over a dry surface quickly is useful for creating texture or sparkle when painting water.

WET-IN-WET
Paint applied to a wet surface will blend freely to create soft effects. The underpainting should be no more than one-third dry or hard edges will form.

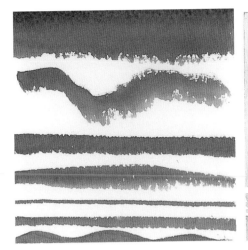
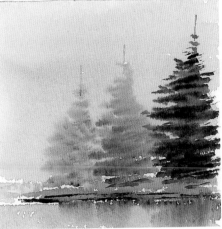
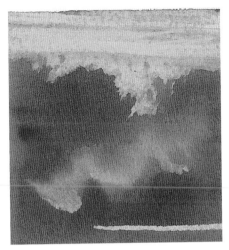

WET ON DRY

Paint applied to a dry surface will create crisp hard edges or dry brush effects. Applying the paint with different pressures will create a range of wide or narrow lines.

DRY ON WET

Varied effects can be achieved by painting a fairly dry paint into a wet underpainting. Soft effects can be achieved, and as the underpainting dries, more detail will result.

SOFT EFFECTS

Paint can be easily removed from a wet underpainting using a clean, moist, absorbent brush. This technique is ideal for creating clouds.

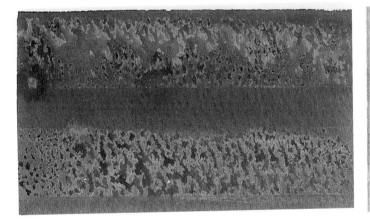
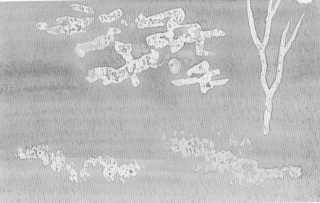

CREATING TEXTURE

Here a piece of masking tape has been pressed over a moist underpainting and then removed. The masking tape will pick up the colour, creating a textured effect that is useful for grass, rocks, tree trunks and many other surfaces.

CREATING SHAPE AND TEXTURE

Here both permanent masking medium and marks made with an oil pastel have acted as a 'resist' that prevents the paint reaching the paper. With permanent masking the medium isn't removed; colour can be added to it if required. The texture is ideal for trees and rocks.

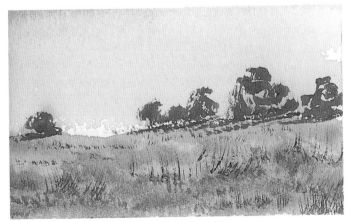

BRUSH WORK

A useful technique for creating the effects of tufts of grass is to fan the hairs of a paint-laden round brush and, holding the brush by the tip of the handle, flick upwards to create the desired effect.

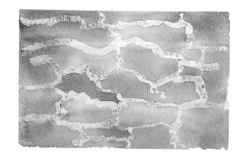

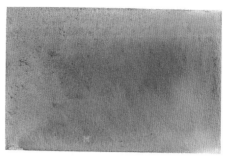

MASKING FLUID

Here masking fluid has been applied to create the effect of mortar between stonework. Masking is removed when the overpainting is dry, using a putty eraser.

GRANULATION MEDIUM

While some watercolour pigments are inherently granular, this medium adds a mottled or granular appearance to colours which usually give a smooth wash.

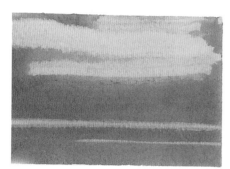

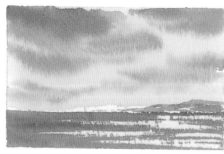

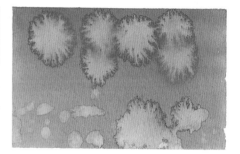

LIFTING PAINT

After wetting a dry underpainting with a clean wet brush, it's possible to remove paint by wiping with an absorbent tissue. By shaping the tissue, various thick or thin lines can be created.

SCRAPING

Sparkle on the water has been achieved by scraping a razor blade over the surface. Care must be taken to ensure the paper surface isn't too badly damaged.

WATER DROPLETS

Water dropped or flicked onto a moist underpainting can create an interesting range of effects.

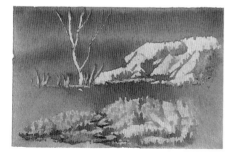

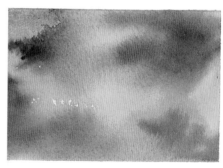

BLENDING

Beautiful effects can be created by brushing moist paint into a very wet underpainting and tilting the surface in different directions, encouraging the pigments to run and blend together – ideal for skies.

PALETTE KNIFE

Various effects can be achieved by moving wet paint with a palette knife, depending on the angle of the knife to the paper and the timing.

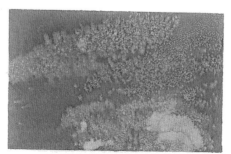

TABLE SALT

Sprinkling table salt over a moist underpainting creates effects that will depend on the wetness of the underpainting. When it is dry, just blow away the salt.

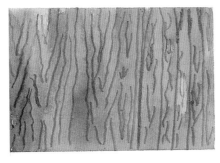

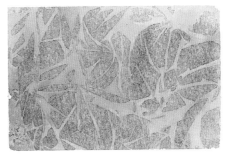

BRUISING

Stroking a cocktail stick through a wet underpainting slightly bruises the paper surface. The wet paint will gather in the indentations, creating the effect of wood grain and other surfaces.

PLASTIC WRAP

Crumple plastic wrap, press it on wet paint and leave to dry. When it is removed the pigment will have varied patterns. Use for the background of a woodland scene or to create a rough foreground.

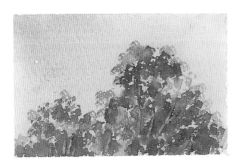

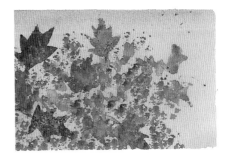

STIPPLING

With a hog hair or other stiff brush, stipple paint to create the effect of tree foliage or rough grass.

SPATTERING

Wet paint flicked or flung over a moist or dry surface creates interesting effects. Use for tree foliage, wild flowers or wherever texture is needed.

IMPRINTING

Various shapes cut from mount card can be dipped in paint and pressed on to a dry underpainting to produce various effects, including leaf shapes.

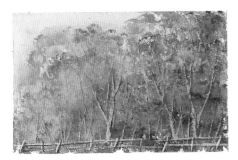

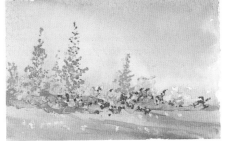

SCRATCHING OUT

In this example, the corner of a palette knife was used to scratch in the tree structures when the paint was about one-third dry. Scratching when the paint is too wet causes bruising of the surface and dark tree structures would result.

OIL PASTEL

Here an oil pastel has been used to represent flowers. Overpainting is repelled by the pastel. The technique is useful for painting garden scenes, veins in leaves, textures on rock, sparkle on water, window frames and other highlights.

SPONGING

Dip a damp sponge into paint and stipple to create tree foliage, foreground texture and so on. A sponge moistened with clean water can be used to wipe across mountain tops and remove paint to represent low cloud or mist.

WATERCOLOUR TECHNIQUES

DESIGN PRINCIPLES

COMPOSITION

Choosing the best viewpoint to give a pleasing composition
is a basic requirement. By composition, we mean the best
arrangement of the elements in the landscape to produce an
attractive painting. This includes several stages; tonal studies of
possible compositions, simplifying the scene by discarding any
details that make no positive contribution to the painting, and
balancing the composition. Selecting the best viewpoint means
the composition can be significantly stronger.

The two examples shown illustrate this point. Instead of looking
at the scene straight on (top), I viewed it from the left, which gave
a much improved representation of the mountains (below). See
pages 42–45 for a detailed analysis of composition.

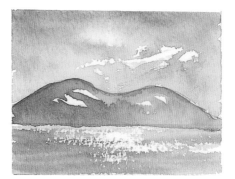

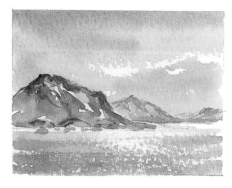

TONAL VALUES

Determining the correct tonal values – that is, the establishment of
light and dark areas in a painting – is crucial if your painting is to
be successful.

The best way of establishing the relationship between the
lightness and darkness of any hue is by constructing a scale; the
example near right progresses from 1 (black) to 10 (white). Using
this information, you can then make a quick tonal sketch to clarify
your thinking before putting paint to paper.

On pages 16–19 you will find more in-depth information about
how tonal values are used.

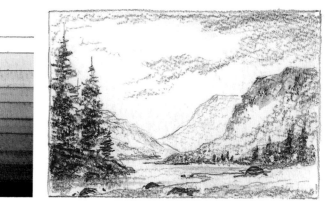

RECESSION

Recession in your painting is a simple matter of producing a
quick tonal study, making elements farthest away pale in tone,
middle distance a middle tone and foreground darker in tone. This
process ensures that the viewer is able to look into the painting
into the distance. Compare the tonal study above with the
completed sketch.

BALANCE

I think of balance in three areas; compositional balance, tonal
balance and colour balance. While the first two are covered in
more detail later in the book, with colour balance it is a matter
of taste. As artists, subtlety is our watchword! In design we try to
create an initial attraction and colour combination that the viewer
can live with over time. A colour balance that works is to contrast
a warm area, say sienna and yellows, with a cold area of, say, cold
blue and green.

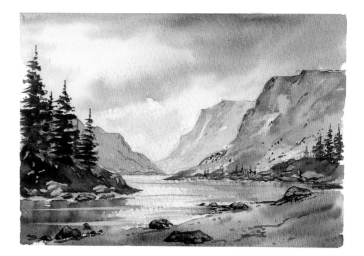

COLOUR MIXING

You will find a very comprehensive section on colour mixing on page 58; this initial look at colour just introduces the fundamental principle that colours have a 'temperature' that affects the viewer's response to a painting.

WARM COLOURS

Warm colours are generally thought of as combinations of yellows, sienna, browns and reds. In the 'doodle' above I have used Cadmium Yellow Pale, Raw Sienna, Burnt Sienna, Burnt Umber and Alizarin Crimson.

COOL COLOURS

In this 'doodle', I have mixed Cadmium Yellow Pale with Cobalt Blue to make green and produced darker tones by adding various quantities of Payne's Grey, which is a cool blue-grey.

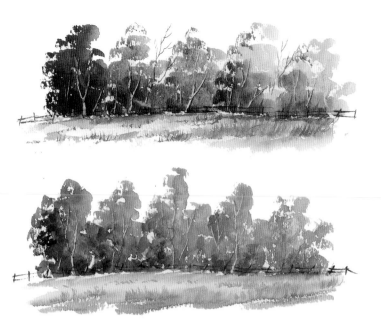

COLOUR COMBINATIONS

More than one hundred shades of green can be produced by mixing combinations of Payne's Grey, Cobalt Blue, Raw Sienna and Cadmium Yellow Pale. Thirty shades of green are shown here. For an extensive range of colour combinations to satisfy most needs, turn to page 58.

TEXTURES

All paintings will show three types of texture.

SMOOTH TEXTURE: Achieved by lightly brushing a well-loaded brush over dry paper.

ROUGH TEXTURE: Achieved by brushing a damp brush quickly over dry paper.

SOFT TEXTURE: Created by using the wet-in-wet technique – brushing with a loaded moist brush into an underpainting that must be less than one-third dry to avoid hard edges. Here, timing is important.

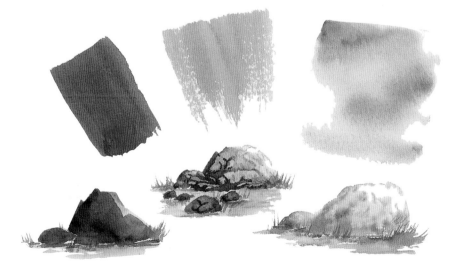

DESIGN PRINCIPLES

HARMONY

Harmony in a painting is achieved by providing small changes between size, shape, line, value/tone, texture or colour. An example of colour harmony can be observed in the sketch on the right. Only two colours have been used here – blue and yellow. The simplest way to achieve colour harmony is to use a limited range of colours. If the aforementioned elements are repeated using great change, the result is contrast. If, however, little change is implemented, the principles of harmony are being observed.

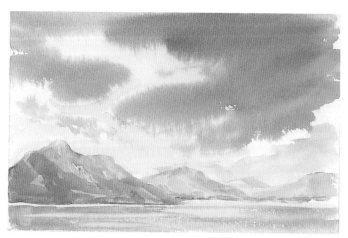

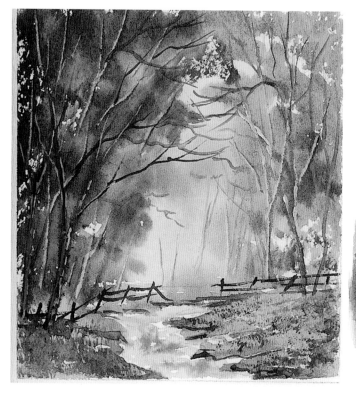

CONTRAST

Contrast comes from an abrupt change from one element to another. In the woodland 'doodle' here, the warm foreground trees on the left contrast with the cool background leading the eye into the distance.

Contrasting colours are those directly opposite each other on the colour wheel – that is, red/green, orange/blue, purple/yellow. Contrast is also derived from the elements of shape, line, value and texture. The term 'counterchange' is widely used to describe the painting of a light object against a dark background, as in the 'doodle' below, or vice versa.

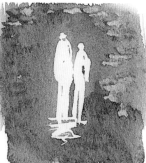

GRADATION

While contrast provides a distinct, sharp change, gradation involves a more gradual change. Skies, for example, represent a gradual change of colour and value. In a group of trees there may be a gradual change between their green foliage and the grass in a meadow that surrounds them.

Gradation occurs in values, colours, shapes, size, line and direction. Gradation in direction – for example, a woodland path that bends from left to right – can be used to lead the eye into the distance or to the focal point.

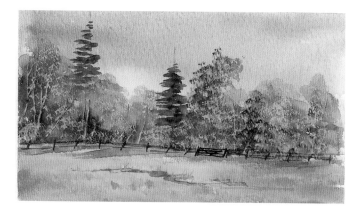

VARIATION

Variation embraces all of the aforementioned principles and involves making changes abruptly, gradually or in a small way to ensure the viewer doesn't become bored. As artists we are entertainers and our job is to produce finished paintings that inspire the viewer. How well we do this distinguishes the professional painter from the amateur.

In the example shown at the top of this page, the roughly made fence looks much more pleasing than a beautifully made fence with perfectly positioned upright posts and three perfectly horizontal bars.

All the elements of contrast, gradation and harmony are evident in this seascape (right).

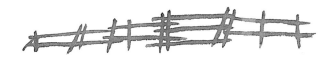

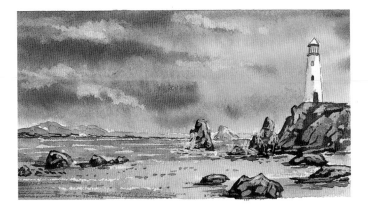

This simple landscape can be done in three stages:

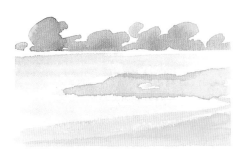

STAGE 1 involves a simple wash.

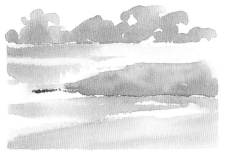

STAGE 2 involves brushing in a darker tone while the underpainting is still wet.

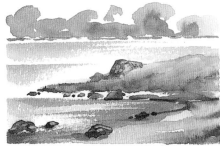

STAGE 3 involves adding darker tones using a less diluted pigment while the underpainting is still less than one-third dry. The colours and tones will fuse together to create a natural-looking grass area.

SHAPE, SIZE, LINE, UNITY

The variety of shapes artists produce all fit into three categories – rectangular, angular or curved. As an artist, you are in the shape-making business, as all paintings will embrace these shapes even if one of these will be dominant.

In a mountainous scene the triangle will be dominant; in a scene with a building, the rectangular shape will be dominant; and in a tree grouping, the circular shape may be dominant. Dominance can be ensured by shape, tonal value or colour. Size and shape can create contrast in a painting, for example a large angular rock contrasting with smaller round rocks.

The direction of line can dominate a painting, too. In a woodland scene, for example, the vertical tree trunks can dominate, creating a sense of awe, while horizontal lines create a sense of peace and tranquillity.

Study the principles of design, and with experience embrace these in your painting. It's better to spend time producing tonal studies to clarify your thinking, rather than rushing in and ruining a perfectly good piece of watercolour paper.

The painting should have unity when it is finished. The colours should be repeated in various values across the painting, with the sky colours being represented in the foreground, and dark, small shapes should balance larger, light shapes. There should be only one focal point so as not to confuse the viewer, and two similar elements should never be placed above or below each other. Study the section on composition on pages 42–45 to progress your understanding further.

DESIGN PRINCIPLES

THE IMPORTANCE OF TONAL STUDIES

I have already touched briefly on the subject of tonal studies. Now I want to put into practice the knowledge I have shared with you by showing you my approach to an upland farmstead from concept to finished painting.

As you have learnt, the arrangement of lights and darks in a painting can contribute more to the success of a painting than any other design principle. In this project my tonal strategy is one of the most important decisions I shall have to make.

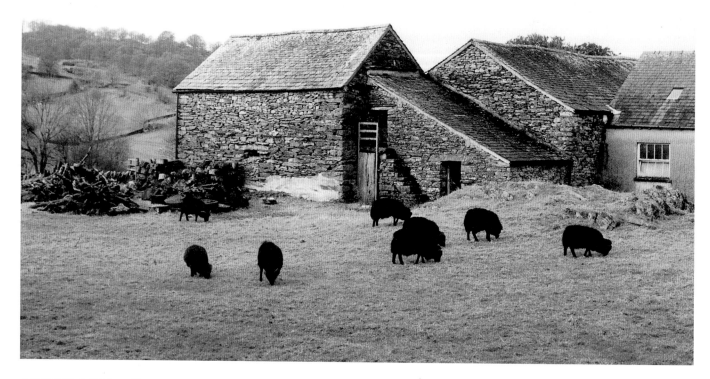

APPROACH – From concept to completed painting

When I visit a location for the first time, I like to view the scene from several vantage points. The information I get from this exercise will determine the best compositions. Some vantage points are quickly ruled out, while others give me an immediate buzz. I look for distinctive features; the focal point or centre of interest, which may be a tree, a large rock, an impressive mountain peak or a figure in the landscape. I discard any elements that won't affect the overall composition by their absence. Don't forget to simplify – you can't compete with nature.

Having selected several possible compositions, I produce a quick tonal value study of each one. These sketches take only a few minutes to complete but will help me think through my approach before I begin my outline drawing or commit to applying colour. As I produce the series of value studies, my concentration is focused on the design principles we looked at earlier and how the tonal values could be incorporated into the composition.

My viewpoints were compromised because of the restrictions imposed by a high hedge and limited access from the road. Using my viewfinder (consisting of an 11.5 × 7.5 cm/4½ × 3 in aperture cut into a 19 × 12.5 cm/7½ × 5 in piece of mounting card), I studied several possibilities closely before finally selecting the composition I found most pleasing. I took several photographs before returning home to begin work in my studio.

There are six possible value patterns that I could use to complete this painting. Let's look at them in turn:

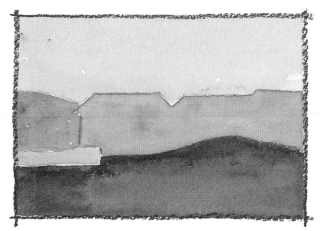

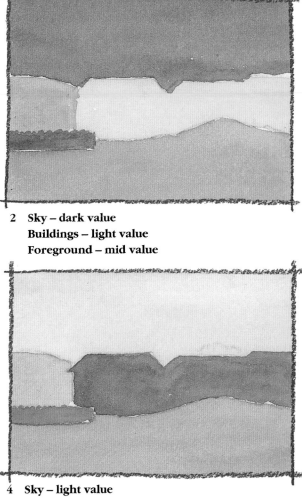

1   Sky – light value
    Buildings – mid value
    Foreground – dark value

2   Sky – dark value
    Buildings – light value
    Foreground – mid value

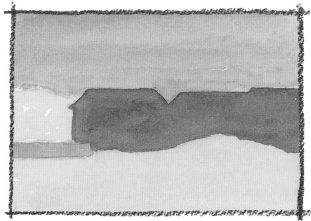

3   Sky – mid value
    Buildings – dark value
    Foreground – light value

4   Sky – light value
    Buildings – dark value
    Foreground – mid value

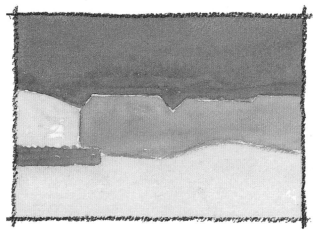

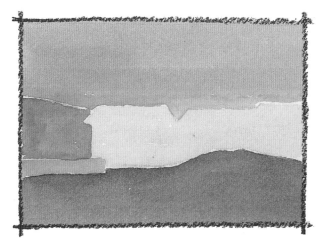

5   Sky – dark value
    Buildings – mid value
    Foreground – light value

6   Sky – mid value
    Buildings – light value
    Foreground – dark value

Any of the six possible tonal value patterns on the previous page would make a successful painting. The aim is to provide contrast/counterchange between each element in the painting, ensuring that each element is distinctive. Examine these value patterns and you will see that lights are placed against darks and darks against lights. Note especially the tonal relationships between the wall and the building.

To complete this landscape, I have basically chosen value pattern number 1 but have varied it slightly by making the wall darker and counterchanging it with a light value in the distant foreground.

Incidentally, the black sheep in the photograph are not indigenous to the area so I have used artistic licence and replaced them with the black-faced sheep one would would expect to see. Always remember that you don't have to reproduce what you can see, either in a photograph or on location.

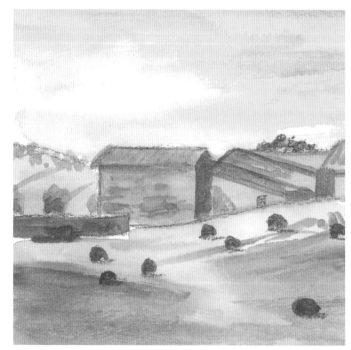

WHAT YOU WILL NEED

PAPER:

640 gsm/300 lb Winsor & Newton Rough

BRUSHES:

Winsor & Newton Sceptre Gold II Series size 14 round, size 3 rigger, ¾in flat, 1½in hake

COLOURS:

Payne's Grey, Cerulean Blue, Alizarin Crimson, Raw Sienna, Burnt Sienna, Sap Green

SUPPORTIVE:

Masking fluid, dark brown water-soluble crayon, gouache or acrylic white paint for sheep, palette knife

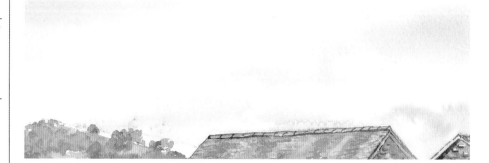

SKY

This was painted wet-in-wet, using the 38 mm/1½ in hake brush.

The sky area was initially washed with a very pale Raw Sienna and when the shine had gone from the underpainting, a stronger mix of Cerulean Blue was brushed in to represent the cloud structures.

DISTANT HILLS AND BUSHES

A pale green wash was applied to represent the distant hills and when dry the bushes and walls were added.

The middle distance bushes were painted with a mix of Sap Green and Burnt Sienna. The depth in the bushes was achieved by adding some Payne's Grey to the mix.

This area of the painting wasn't completed until the buildings and broken-down stone wall had been added.

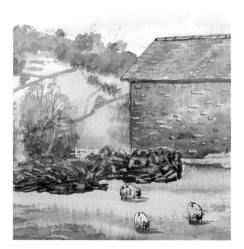

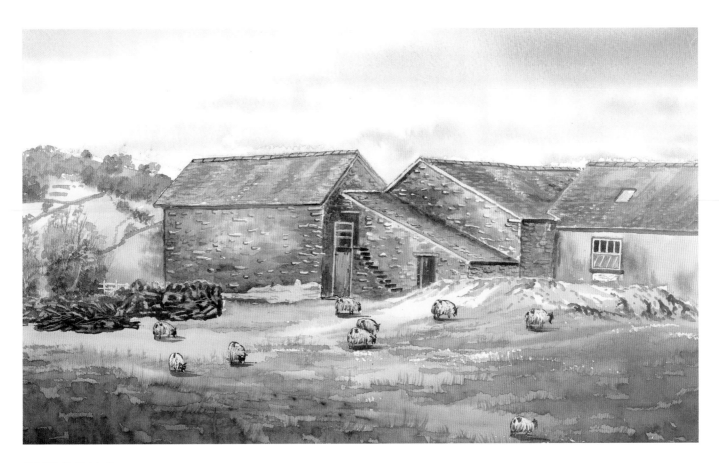

BUILDINGS

Care was taken to draw the buildings to scale and in relation to each other. A Payne's Grey/Alizarin Crimson mix was applied to the roofs in various light and dark values to indicate weathering. The rigger brush was then used to put in a few tile shapes in lighter values.

The 19 mm/¾ in flat brush was used to paint the walls by applying an initial Raw Sienna wash, followed by the selective addition of Burnt Sienna. A palette knife was used to move paint when it was approximately one-third dry to represent areas of lighter-toned stonework.

The doorframes, handrail at the top of the stairs and the window frames were initially masked prior to applying paint.

FOREGROUND GRASS AND SHEEP

The foreground grass was painted by initially applying a Raw Sienna wash over the whole of the grass area and adding darker tones of Sap Green/Burnt Sienna mix at varying stages, flicking upwards with the corner of the hake to indicate the tufts of rough grass.

The sheep were finally painted, taking care to follow the principles of design and avoid placing them at equal distances or in straight lines. See page 117 for painting sheep.

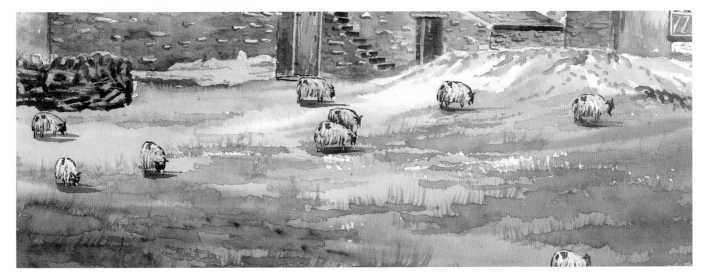

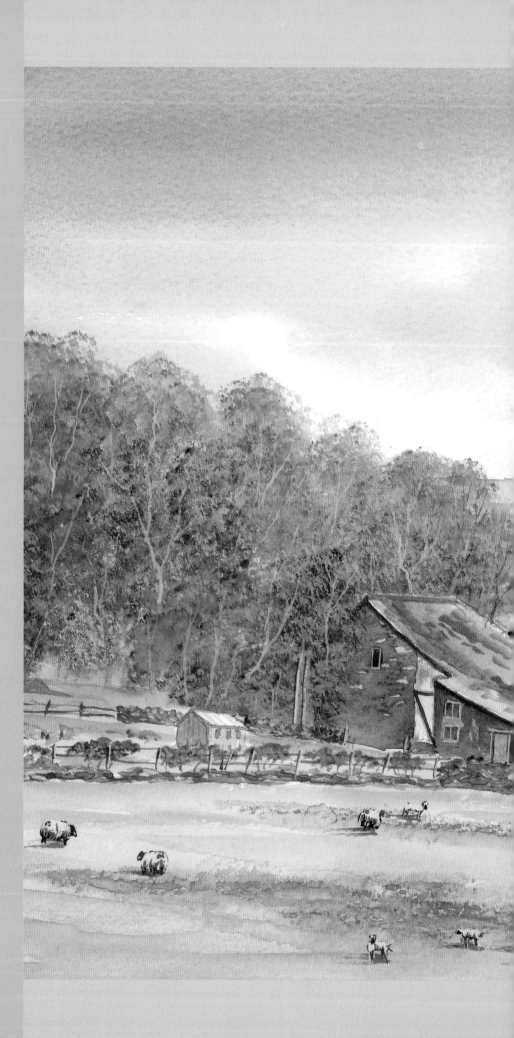

Right: Lambing Time

SPRING

The Spring comes in with all hues and smells
In freshness, breathing over hills and dells
O'er woods where May her gorgeous drapery flings
And meads washed fragrant by their laughing springs
Fresh are new open'd flowers, untouched and free
From the bold rifling of the amorous bee
The happy time of singing birds is come
And love's lone pilgrimage now finds a home;
Among the mossy oaks now coos the dove
And hoarse crow finds softer notes for love.

John Clare

In Spring the earth seems to be reborn; new shoots push through as soon as the ice and snow have melted. Fresh green grass appears and dormant buds grow fatter, waiting to burst into leaf at the first opportunity. Lambs play in the fields, while the rooks gather in the treetops and daffodils sway in the breeze.

The birds are beginning to build their nests and the dawn chorus reaches a crescendo each morning as the days begin to lengthen. Everything appears clean and fresh. Frequent showers and warmer temperatures stimulate new growth, and the air smells sweet. Spring, one of my favourite times of year, marks the beginning of the artist's year.

SPRING SNOW – PROJECT

The photograph below was taken on Thurstaston Hill, a few miles from my home in north-west England. The area is a popular beauty spot overlooking the Dee Estuary, and is one of my favourite places to walk. It is riddled with woodland paths and is famous for its red sandstone rocks which are characteristic of this region.

It is said that the great artist JMW Turner visited Thurstaston to capture in paint the wonderful sunsets that can be seen here. The views from the Hill are breathtaking in all directions. The photograph makes a pleasing composition, although the painting was in fact completed a little earlier, before the fall of snow began to melt.

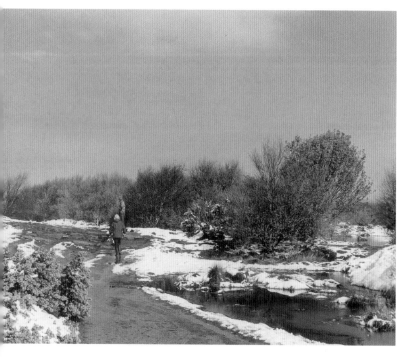

The tonal study became the plan for the painting. Although such a study can be produced in only a few minutes, it provides thinking time to establish one's approach to the final painting.

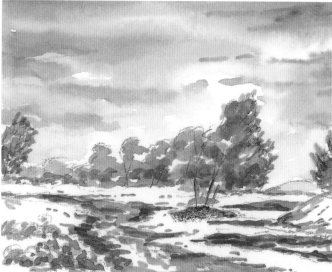

WHAT YOU WILL NEED

PAPER:
Winsor & Newton 640 gsm/300 lb Rough

BRUSHES:
Winsor & Newton Sceptre Gold II Series size 14 round, size 3 rigger, 38 mm/1½ in hake, 13 mm/½ in round hog hair brush

COLOURS:
Payne's Grey, Cerulean Blue, Alizarin Crimson, Raw Sienna, Burnt Sienna, Burnt Umber, Sap Green, Cadmium Yellow Deep

SUPPORTIVE:
Masking fluid, white acrylic paint, tissues (toilet roll), dark brown water-soluble crayon

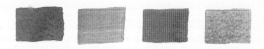

STAGE 1:
DRAWING AND MASKING
A rough outline drawing was completed using a dark brown water-soluble crayon. The areas to be reserved to represent snow were masked.

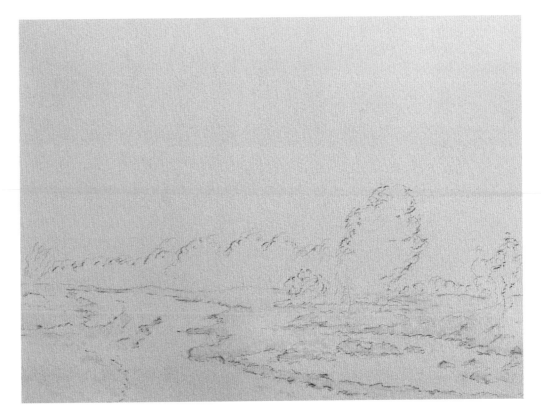

STAGE 2:
SKY
The sky was a soft Cerulean Blue, applied with the hake brush over a Raw Sienna underpainting applied to wet the paper. A very small quantity of Payne's Grey was added to the Cerulean Blue to produce slightly darker values of blue at the top of the sky and in selected areas. A tissue was used to remove colour by dabbing to create white clouds.

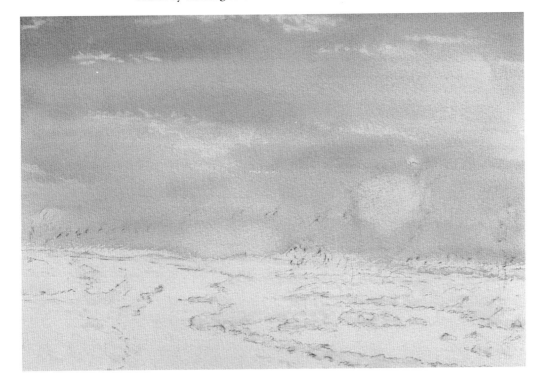

SPRING SNOW – PROJECT

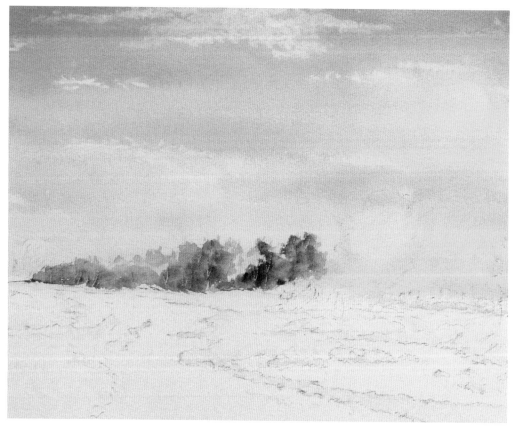

STAGE 3:
DISTANT BUSHES

The side of the size 14 round brush was used to twitch downwards from the top of the bushes to establish their mass. Raw Sienna and Payne's Grey were used to produce various tonal values. A quick twitch of the brush combined with a light touch is what is needed.

STAGE 4:
DISTANT TREES AND PATHS

Using the same technique and colour combinations described in Stage 3, the large trees were positioned. A touch of Burnt Sienna was added to the trees to provide colour variation and a cocktail stick was used to scratch in the tree structure while the paint was still wet.

The size 14 round brush loaded with the Cerulean Blue wash was used to represent water in the pools and on the paths. The distant hills were then painted.

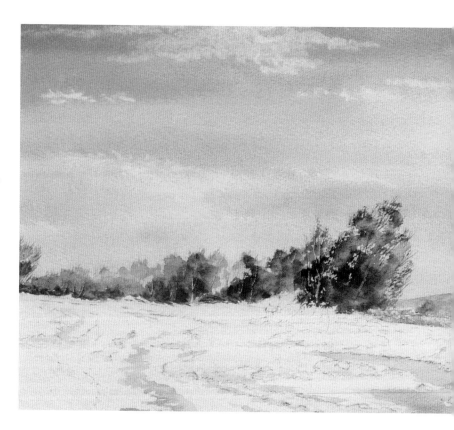

SPRING

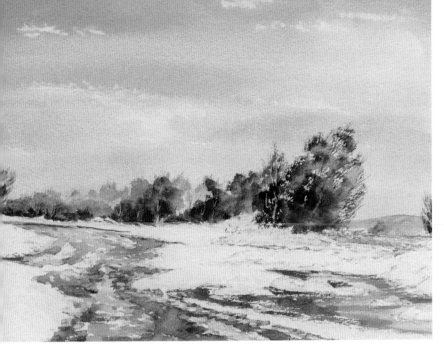

STAGE 5:
PATH AND FOREGROUND POOL

A Burnt Sienna/Burnt Umber mix was used to paint the paths. Payne's Grey was added to Cerulean Blue to create depth in the pool and to provide definition to the edges of the paths.

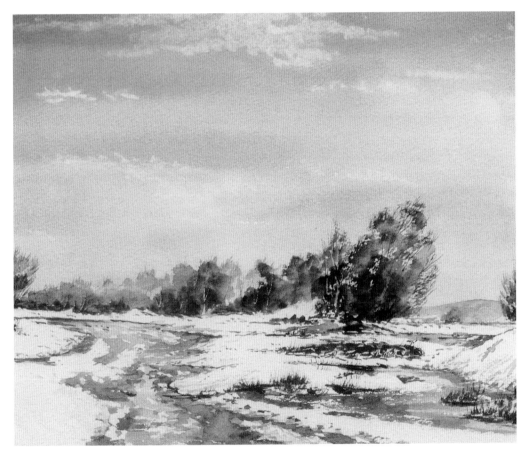

STAGE 6:
ROUGH GRASSES

The land areas that weren't covered by snow, including the tufts of grass, were painted using the size 14 round brush. To paint the tufts of grass, load the brush with a Burnt Sienna wash, fan the hairs of the brush between the thumb and forefinger, hold the brush by its tip and twitch upwards - easy and effective. The masking was removed by gently rubbing with a putty eraser and then a few cloud shadows were painted with a size 6 brush loaded with Cerulean Blue.

SPRING SNOW – PROJECT

KEY POINTS

1 Remember the golden rule that a detailed foreground demands a simple sky to avoid the painting becoming too fussy.

2 Take care to ensure your drawing accurately represents the scene. Take particular care with the angles of the path.

3 Add depth to your painting by the application of darker values in the path, tree and water.

4 If you can, take a snippet of gorse and match your colour to it.

5 A painting must be a completed unit. To achieve this, colours, textures, shapes and so on should be repeated in areas of the painting. Splashes of Burnt Sienna, for example, have been echoed in the distant trees, gorse, path and tufts of grass, while the sky colours are reflected in the pool and path. Remember to apply the principles of design (see pages 12–15), including variation, gradation, contrast and harmony.

STAGE 7:

GORSE BUSHES

Gorse bushes vary in colour from a soft yellow to deep yellow, depending on the soil in which they are growing and the length of time that they have been in flower.

It's a good idea to take a small cutting and compare it with the colour you hope to use to paint them. In this case, I found that Cadmium

Yellow Deep was the exact colour. The underpainting was a mix of Burnt Sienna and Sap Green. A little white acrylic paint was added to the Cadmium Yellow Deep to ensure the flowers remained sharp and the colour did not soak into the watercolour underpainting, which would have resulted in a blurred representation.

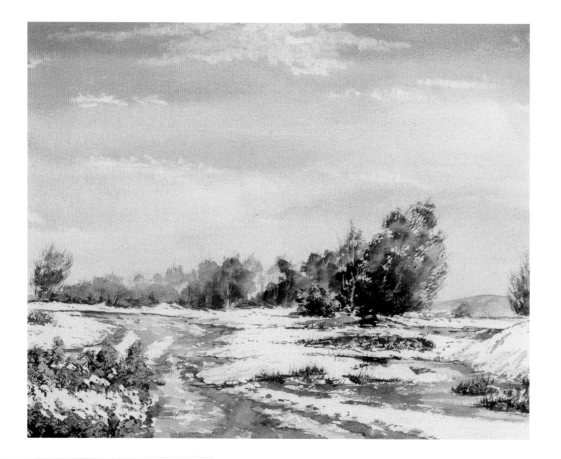

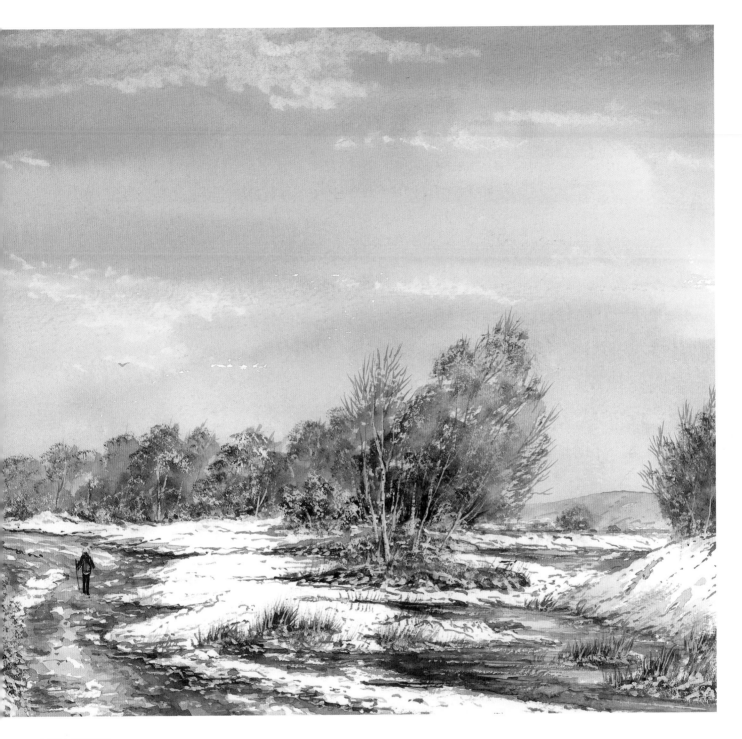

FINAL STAGE:
ADDING THE DETAILS

My normal practice is never to complete a painting in one sitting. I like to look at the painting over a period of several days - it's amazing what you failed to see in your first effort. Using the rigger brush loaded with a white acrylic paint and a little Raw Sienna, I have painted in some tree structures. I have added more detail in the path and painted the walkers (just the shape of a lemon for a body, two legs that touch at the feet, a small head and add a rucksack, stick and so on). It's as easy as that. Finally I have used the hog hair brush to stipple a little white acrylic paint into the foliage to represent snow and added a few birds on the left. I hope you enjoyed painting this one.

SPRING SNOW – PROJECT

GREEN HARMONY –
CLOSE UP

There are many shades of green in this painting, providing you with an opportunity to practise colour mixing.

BACKGROUND

It's important to ensure that the background does not detract from the more detailed right-hand tree group and the foreground.

A weak Cerulean Blue/Sap Green wash was applied using a 38 mm/1½ in hake brush and while the paper was moist, darker tones of Sap Green/Payne's Grey were brushed into selected areas to establish a soft, varied background. While it was wet a cocktail stick was used to scratch in a few tree structures. Once it was dry a moist sponge was used to stipple impressions of foliage, using mixes made from Cadmium Yellow Pale/Sap Green and a little white acrylic paint.

SPECIMEN TREE GROUPING

A moist sponge dipped into mixes of Cadmium Yellow Pale/Sap Green was used to create the groups of foliage. It's important not to squeeze the sponge as the paint is stippled. While still wet, some tree structures were scratched in and when dry a Payne's Grey/Burnt Umber mix was used to add tree structures with the rigger brush.

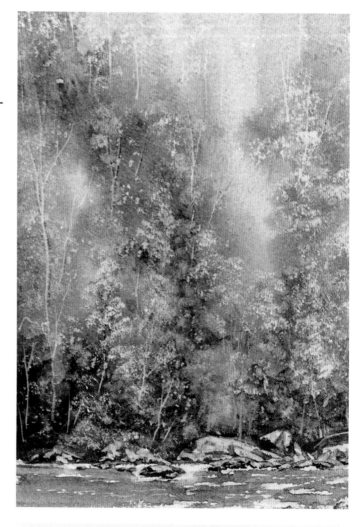

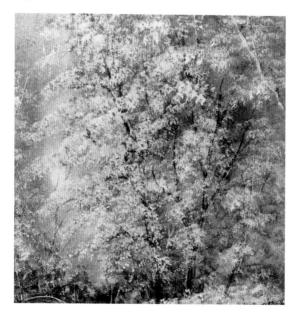

WHAT YOU WILL NEED

PAPER:
640 gsm/300 lb Saunders Waterford Rough

BRUSHES:
Winsor & Newton Sceptre Gold II Series size 14 round, size 3 rigger, 19 mm/¾ in flat, 38 mm/1½ in hake, 13 mm/½ in round hog hair

COLOURS:
Payne's Grey, Cerulean Blue, Raw Sienna, Burnt Sienna, Burnt Umber, Cadmium Yellow Pale, Sap Green

SUPPORTIVE:
Palette knife, white acrylic paint, natural sponge

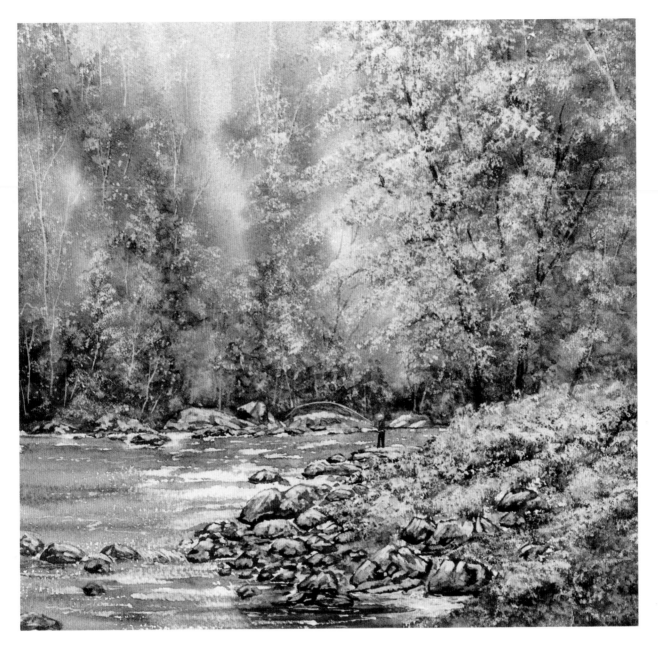

FOREGROUND GRASS AND FOLIAGE

A dark background was underpainted using a Payne's Grey/Sap Green mix and when dry an old hog hair brush was used to stipple in a representation of rough growth. To create sparkle on the foreground, a little white acrylic was added to the Cadmium Yellow Pale/Sap Green mix.

WATER

The water was painted by applying horizontal strokes of a Payne's Grey/Cerulean Blue mix with the side of the size 14 round brush, taking care to leave some white of the paper uncovered.

ROCKS

The rocks were created with the 19 mm/¾ in flat brush, first with a Raw Sienna wash, followed by Burnt Umber and Payne's Grey for depth. When approximately one-third dry, a palette knife was used to move paint, creating realistic-looking rocks.

FISHERMAN

This was painted last, using the rigger brush. Take care not to paint the figure too full-bodied, with short legs and a large head. Keep it simple.

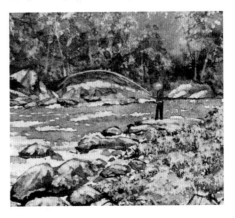

GREEN HARMONY – CLOSE UP

THE BLUEBELL WOOD – PROJECT

Bluebell woods are one of the wonders of nature. The violet-blue carpet of flowers shimmers in the spring sunlight and thrives in the moist atmosphere of temperate woodlands.

Bluebells spread very slowly; a concentrated area of these delightful plants generally signifies the site of ancient deciduous woodland. Fortunately these poisonous plants are not eaten by the deer that tend to frequent the areas where bluebells are found.

There are few more joyous sights than a thick carpet of bluebells illuminated by shafts of sunlight piercing a woodland canopy. When I see this I know that nature has fully awakened from her winter hibernation.

I found the bluebell wood of my study less than 3 km/2 miles from my home. I used photographs as a guide only. The tonal study shown beneath the reference photograph below was the real starting point.

I wanted to include a path that led through the woodland to direct the eye of the viewer into the painting.

WHAT YOU WILL NEED

PAPER:
Winsor & Newton 640 gsm/300 lb Rough

BRUSHES:
Winsor & Newton Sceptre Gold II Series 19 mm/¾ in flat, size 3 rigger, 38 mm/1½ in hake, 19 mm/¾ in round hog hair

COLOURS:
Payne's Grey, Cobalt Blue, Raw Sienna, Burnt Sienna, Cadmium Yellow Pale, Sap Green

SUPPORTIVE:
Palette knife, natural sponge, white acrylic paint, dark brown water-soluble crayon

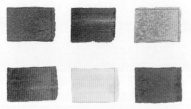

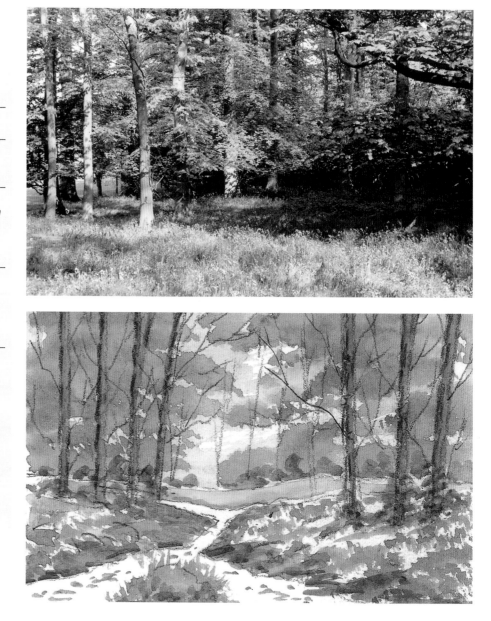

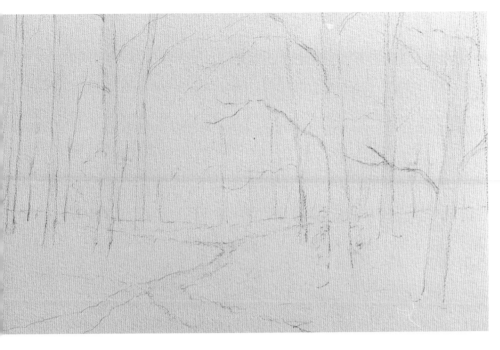

STAGE 1:
DRAWING AND MASKING
The outline shapes of the trees and path were drawn using a dark brown water-soluble crayon. Masking fluid was applied to these areas and also to selected areas of the foreground using a rigger brush. The masking was allowed to dry completely.

STAGE 2:
BACKGROUND
Using the 38 mm/1½ in hake, the sky area was washed with a pale Raw Sienna. Cobalt Blue was brushed in using downward strokes to create an atmospheric background sky. While it was still wet, I used the hake loaded with mixes of Cobalt Blue and Sap Green to brush in rough tree shapes which blended in, providing a background for further detail to be added later.

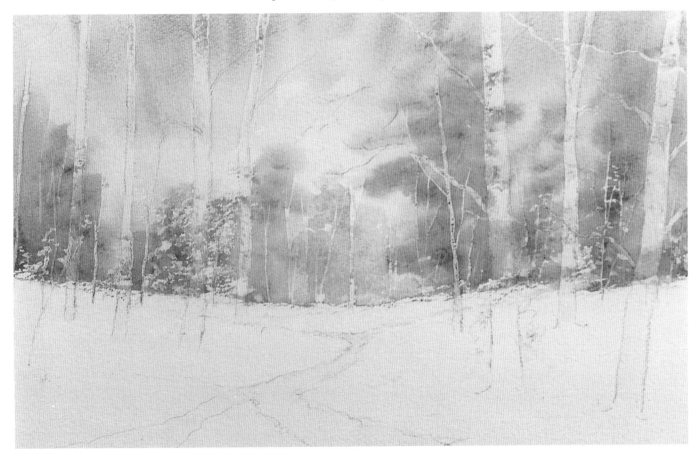

THE BLUEBELL WOOD – PROJECT

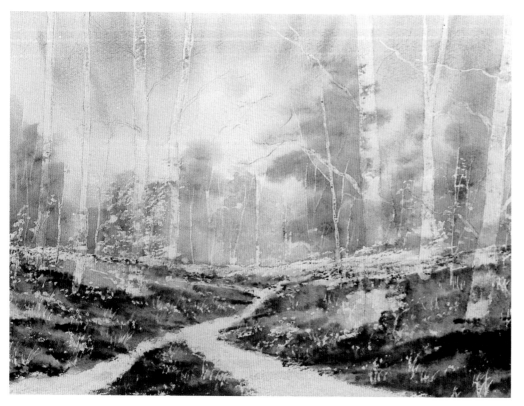

STAGE 3:

FOREGROUND WASHES
With the hake brush loaded with Sap Green, various toned washes were applied. Payne's Grey was added to the Sap Green to give depth here and there. Note how the masking fluid which repels the watercolour shows through.

STAGE 4:

REMOVE MASKING
Using a putty eraser, the dry masking fluid was removed from the trees and bushes.

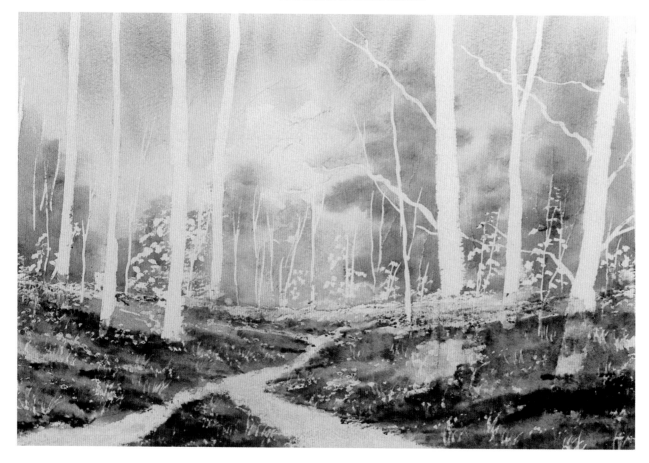

SPRING

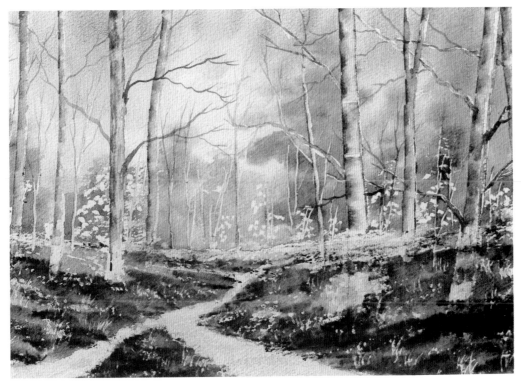

STAGE 5:
TREE STRUCTURES

The tree trunks were painted using the 19 mm/¾ in flat brush by initially applying a weak Raw Sienna wash, followed by a little Burnt Sienna to create variation in the bark. When the paint was approximately one-third dry, darker tones were added to represent shadows.

STAGE 6:
FOLIAGE

The foliage was painted with varying tones of Cadmium Yellow Pale and Sap Green. A natural sponge was used to stipple colour – darker values on the left, lighter values on the right.

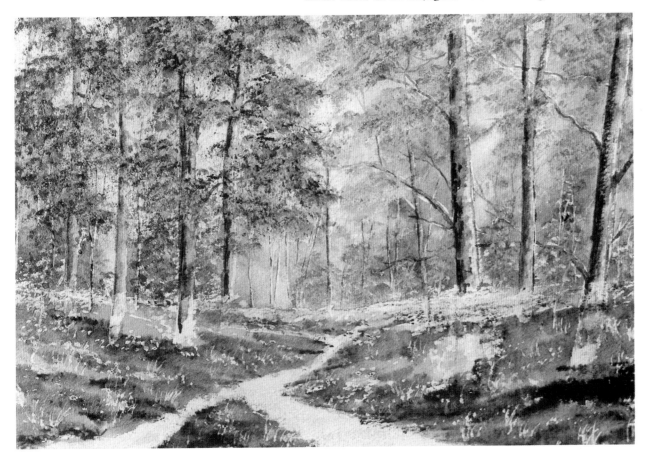

THE BLUEBELL WOOD – PROJECT

KEY POINTS

1 Mask your trees before applying the background washes.

2 Draw the outlines with a dark brown water-soluble crayon, because as paint is applied the crayon washes out – pencil marks will spoil a finished painting.

3 Use a natural sponge to create the foliage, but don't squeeze it as you will lose definition if you do so.

4 Paint the tree trunks wet-in-wet.

5 Paint the edges of the path to look naturally uneven – never with straight lines – and shape them to vanish into the distance.

STAGE 7:

BLUEBELLS

Cobalt Blue was used to provide the background colour for the bluebells and to establish their distribution over the foreground. The masking was removed from the foreground base of the trees and the trunks were painted to ground level.

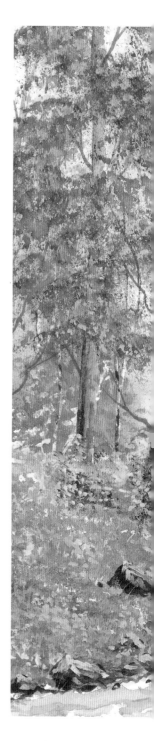

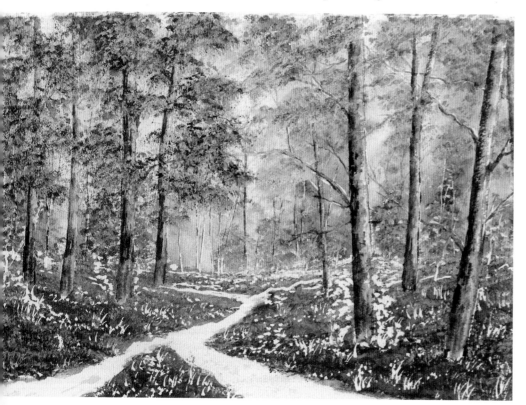

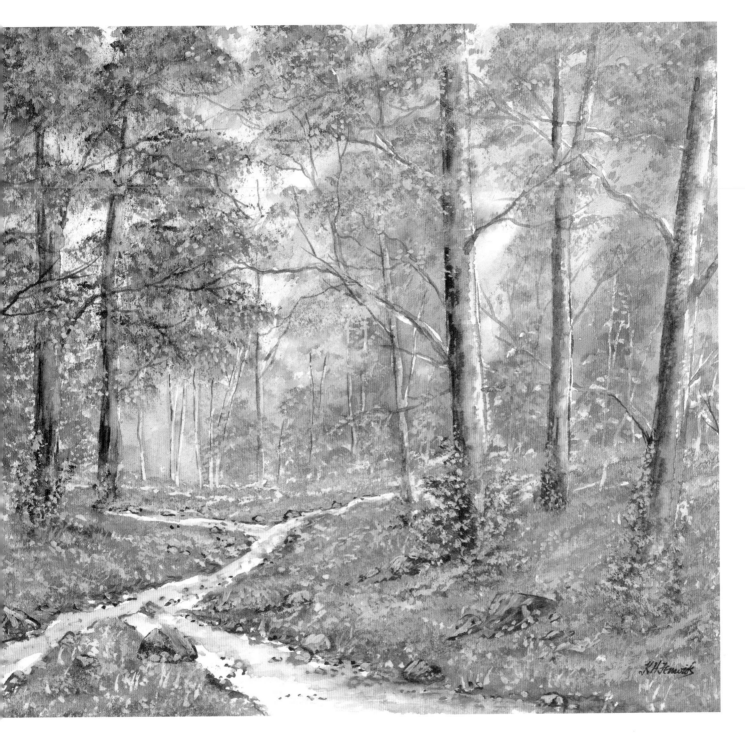

FINAL STAGE:

DETAIL

The carpet of bluebells was completed; the tones vary, with lighter values in the distance and highlights in selected areas. These were stippled in using a hog hair brush. The paler values were achieved by adding a little white acrylic paint to the Cobalt Blue. The small bushes at the base of the trees were added and some tree foliage was highlighted to make a more pleasing composition.

A few additional branches were painted. The masking was removed from the path and a Raw Sienna wash was overpainted with a little Burnt Sienna. Rocks were painted to improve the composition, using a 19 mm/¾ in flat brush, and knifed out to provide realism to their appearance.

Note: Bluebell colours vary significantly between regional areas; they may be bright blue, soft blue or even a violet blue. It's a good idea to pick one and match the colour to it. I find Cobalt Blue is usually the most appropriate colour, but sometimes I need to add a little Alizarin Crimson or even white to vary the values and colours.

THE BLUEBELL WOOD – PROJECT

ULLSWATER DAFFODILS
– CLOSE UP

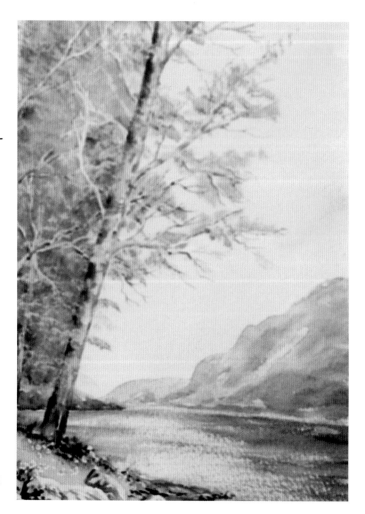

Ullswater is one of the most beautiful sights in the English Lake District. It was the famous Romantic poet William Wordsworth who publicized its charms, most notably in his poem 'Daffodils', written in 1804:

I wandered lonely as a cloud,

That floats on high o'er vales and hills,

When all at once I saw a crowd,

A host, of golden daffodils;

Beside the lake, beneath the trees,

Fluttering and dancing in the breeze.

Ullswater is one of my favourite painting spots. It is a joy to behold at any season of the year but best of all in the springtime.

WHAT YOU WILL NEED

PAPER:
Winsor & Newton 640 gsm/300 lb Rough

BRUSHES:
Winsor & Newton Sceptre Gold II Series size 14 round, size 6 round, size 3 rigger, 19 mm/¾ in flat, 38 mm/1½ in hake

COLOURS:
Payne's Grey, Cerulean Blue, Raw Sienna, Burnt Sienna, Burnt Umber, Cadmium Yellow Pale, Cadmium Yellow Deep, Sap Green

SUPPORTIVE:
Masking fluid, sponge, palette knife, tissues

TREES

Masking fluid was used to preserve the white of the paper necessary for the tree structures. When dry, the background was painted by applying washes of Raw Sienna and Sap Green with the hake brush. At ground level Burnt Umber was washed in to create depth. When completely dry the masking was removed and the tree structures painted. A pale Raw Sienna was applied using a 19 mm/¾ in flat brush and darker values of Burnt Umber were painted to create variation. Finally, impressions of clumps of foliage were painted by stippling light values of a soft green, produced by adding a little white acrylic paint to a mix of Sap Green/Cadmium Yellow Deep. A sponge was used to stipple paint.

MOUNTAINS AND WATER

The mountains were painted using sweeping strokes of the hake brush from peak to ground level.

The distant mountains were painted in pale blue, with some Sap Green and Burnt Sienna added for the larger mountain.

The sparkle on the water was created using the dry brush technique; a light quick stroke with the side of the size 14 round brush, commencing with Cerulean Blue and adding a little Payne's Grey for the darker values was my choice.

The sky was a simple Cerulean Blue using the hake brush.

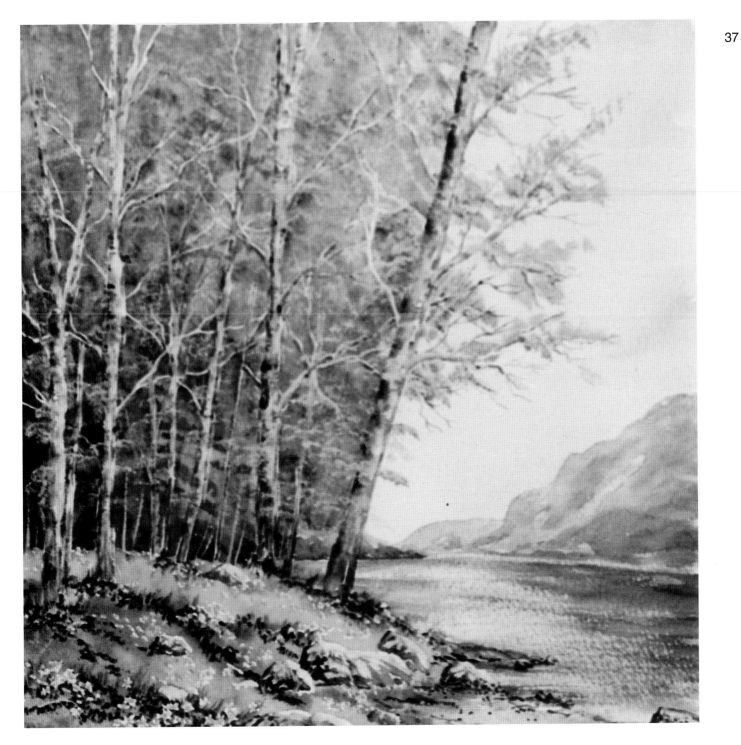

FOREGROUND

The areas to be preserved for the rocks and daffodils were masked. The daffodils were masked by crumpling a tissue to a point, dipping it in masking fluid and stippling. To ensure differing sizes and a variety of shapes of flowers, the size of the pointed tissue and the pressure applied to the watercolour paper with the soaked tissue were important.

When the masking was completely dry, soft yellow green washes were applied, mixed from combinations of Sap Green and Cadmium Yellow Pale. Darker values were painted in to selected areas by adding a little Burnt Umber.

The masking was removed from the foreground. Using a size 6 round brush, Cadmium Yellow Deep was applied to the white of the paper to indicate the daffodils. A rigger brush was used to paint the stems of the flowers.

Raw Sienna was used to define the water's edge and to wash in the rocks. Darker tones of Burnt Umber/Burnt Sienna were used to indicate shadows on the rocks and their form and structure were created by removing paint with a palette knife.

MOONLIGHT
– PROJECT

I return repeatedly to my favourite places and always find something new to inspire me. On an evening walk around the shores of Derwentwater in the English Lake District I was fascinated by the moonlight shimmering across the lake, and couldn't wait to capture the effect. The painting was completed in my studio, using the value study shown and a photograph taken at the time.

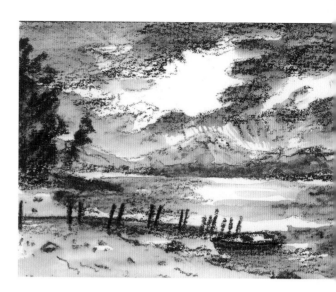

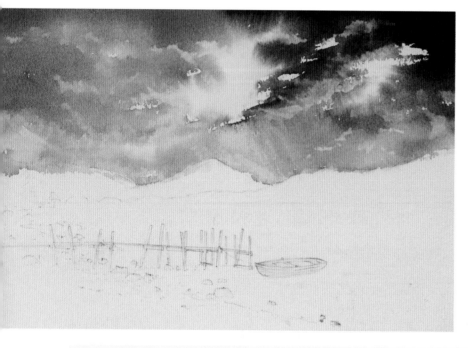

STAGE 1:

DRAWING AND SKY

The outline drawing was completed using a dark brown water-soluble crayon. The sky is the important feature in this painting and needs a little thought before applying paint. To create the effect I wanted, I decided to initially wet the paper with clean water so that I could paint a wet-in-wet sky but, as can be seen, I left small areas of the paper uncovered. I quickly painted the areas of Raw Sienna followed by Cerulean Blue near to the horizon and less dilute mixes of Payne's Grey/Alizarin Crimson above the Cerulean Blue. The board was lifted and tilted, allowing the paint to run together, taking care to leave the areas of Raw Sienna uncovered. Finally, the board was laid flat and with a tissue, a few light clouds were blotted out.

WHAT YOU WILL NEED

PAPER:

Winsor & Newton 640 gsm/300 lb Rough

BRUSHES:

Winsor & Newton Sceptre Gold II Series size 14 round, size 6 round, size 3 rigger, 38 mm/1½ in hake

COLOURS:

Payne's Grey, Cerulean Blue, Alizarin Crimson, Raw Sienna, Burnt Sienna, Sap Green

SUPPORTIVE:

Palette knife, masking fluid

STAGE 2:
MOUNTAINS

Using the hake brush, I painted the distant mountains in lighter tones to ensure recession. When applying paint, it's important that the brush strokes follow the structure of the mountain, from peak to ground level.

Initially, I applied a little masking fluid to create a few highlights. When dry, I overpainted the area with Raw Sienna washes and then followed on by adding mixes of Burnt Sienna and Payne's Grey/Alizarin Crimson. A size 14 round brush was used for the variation in tone and detail. When dry, the masking was removed with a putty eraser and a pale Raw Sienna wash was applied with a size 6 round brush, to represent moonlight reflecting over the peaks.

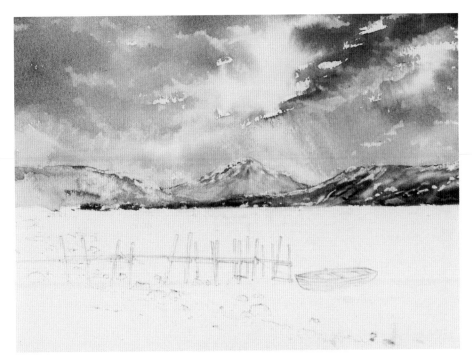

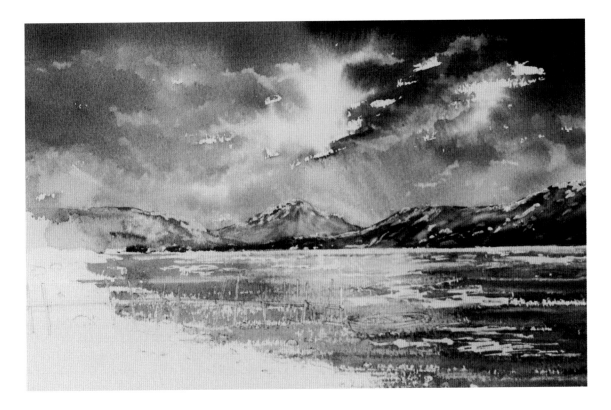

STAGE 3:
MASKING AND WATER

Masking fluid was applied to the landing stage, the boat and highlights on the lake's surface. With the sky colours, washes were applied using the side of the size 14 round brush. Take care when applying the reflected colours from the sky. These must be accurately distributed in the water.

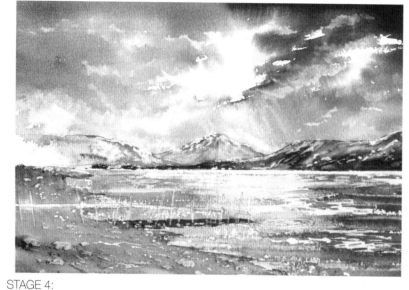

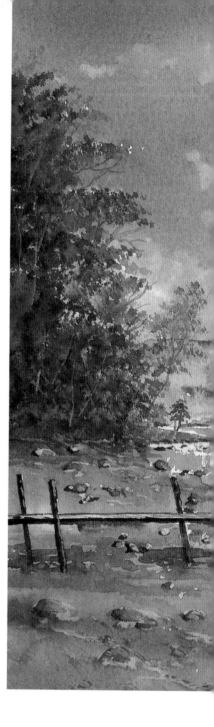

STAGE 4:
SHORELINE

Sweeping strokes with the hake brush initially loaded with a pale Raw Sienna were applied. This was followed by Burnt Sienna over selected areas and a Payne's Grey/ Alizarin Crimson mix added to give darker values over areas where the rocks were to be painted.

Darker values of the Payne's Grey/Alizarin Crimson mix were painted under the landing stage for shadow effect. When the paint was approximately one-third dry a palette knife was used to move paint to give the impression of rocks and boulders in the foreground.

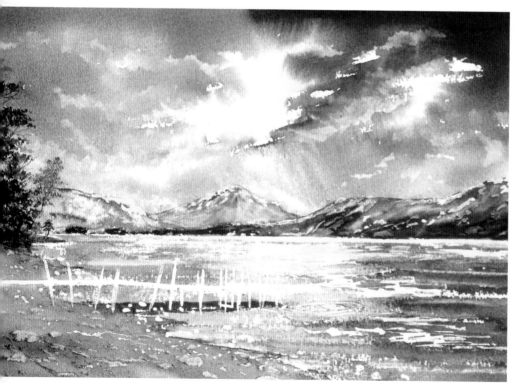

STAGE 5:
REMOVAL OF MASKING

Use a putty eraser to remove the masking fluid from the landing stage. This method of removal is ideal as being soft, the eraser doesn't damage the paper and readily adheres to the masking.

The left-hand trees were painted using a stippling action with a well-worn, round hog hair brush.

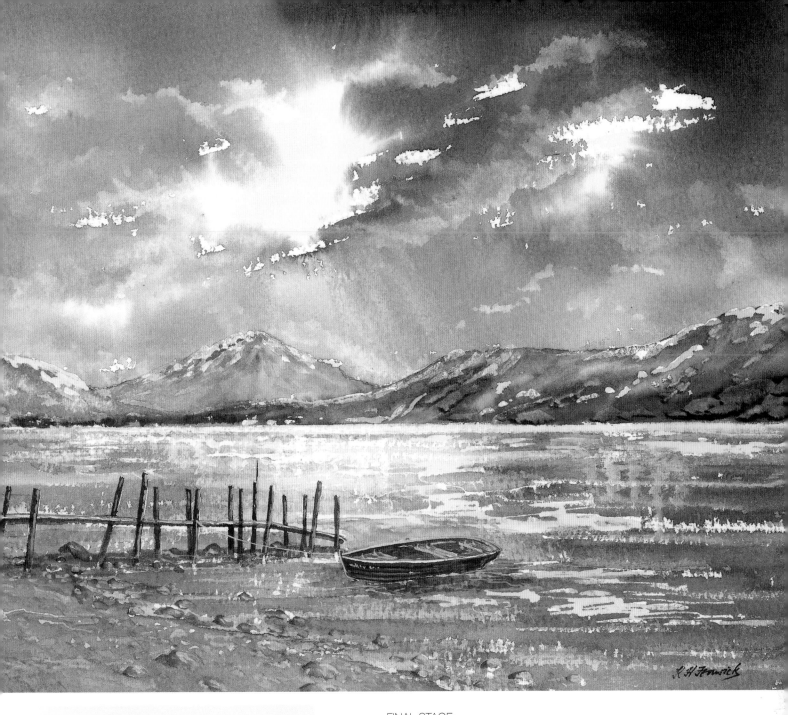

KEY POINTS

1 Take care when painting the wet-in-wet sky. When tilting the board, do not allow the paint to run over the light area that is to show the moonlight.

2 Ensure a pale line is preserved between the land and the water. This is always visible when painting distant water.

3 When painting boats, make sure they are in proportion. The usual error is to make them too wide in relation to their length.

4 To ensure harmony, the sky colours should be reflected in all areas of the painting.

5 Don't forget to paint shadows under the landing stage, the boat and the trees and rocks.

FINAL STAGE:

BOAT AND LANDING STAGE

The masking was removed from the boat and the boat was painted, using Raw Sienna, Burnt Sienna and Payne's Grey. Highlights on the boat and the mooring line were added, using the rigger brush and a little white acrylic paint. The landing stage was painted also using the rigger brush.

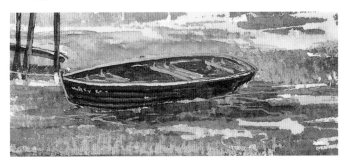

MOONLIGHT – PROJECT

COMPOSITION

Composition can be said to be the process of arranging all the elements in a painting to make a unified whole that is pleasing to the viewer. When we first begin painting we simply want to copy what is in front of us, but in order to create a good composition it may be necessary to move the elements around or use counterchange or scale to highlight a particular feature that leads the viewer's eye into the painting. A centre of interest or focal point is needed, but it isn't always necessary to paint exactly what we see.

We may need to make one tree larger or darker in value, to add a splash of colour or to counterchange it with its background to direct the eye to it. For example, in a river scene the foliage of trees on each side of the river may have the same tonal value and colour. For the painting to work, it may be necessary to make the foreground tree on the left of the painting darker in value than it actually appears and to make the right-hand trees gradually lighter in values as they disappear into the distance. The eye is led down the river and out of the painting behind the dark-value tree in the left-hand foreground. Artistic licence is necessary for the painting to be aesthetically acceptable.

THE CENTRE OF INTEREST, OR FOCAL POINT

This point must be a dominant feature. It may be a dark colourful figure against a light background, an interesting shape or a large dominating feature, such as a tree or church steeple.

The first thing to be decided upon is where the centre of interest is to be positioned. It should never be in the centre or at the extreme edges of a painting. Ideally, the centre of interest should be placed at unequal distances from each edge of the paper.

Artists have developed suitable methods for positioning their centre of interest or focal point. Two such approaches are shown. They are basically similar; the choice is yours. The focal point should ideally be placed at A, B C or D, depending on whether you are looking up or down on the subject.

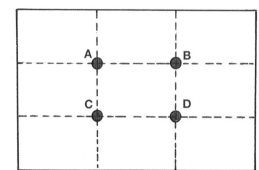

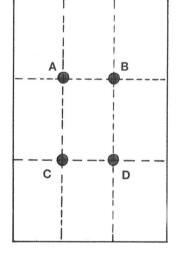

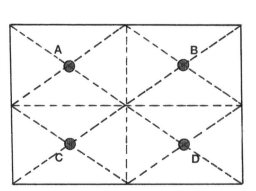

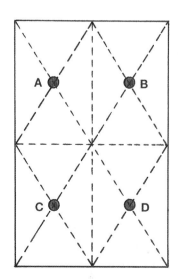

Possible focal points for a good composition

RIGHT AND WRONG COMPOSITIONS

Experience has taught me that some compositions look right and others don't. I'm going to show you some of the pitfalls to avoid. No matter how successful you are at applying paint, if your composition is lacking, your painting won't look right.

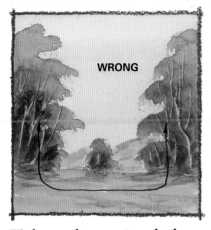

'U' shape – there are trees both sides and centre

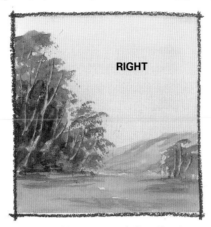

Improved by a varied distribution of trees

1 'U' shape

This is a poor composition, with trees at both sides and one in the middle. It is much more pleasing to show a larger group on one side and a smaller group on the opposite side.

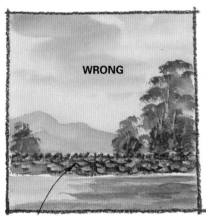

A continuous wall conveys the message 'don't enter my picture'

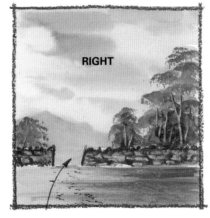

An opening in the wall improves the composition

2 Continuous wall, hedge or fence

For example, by painting a wall right across the painting, the message you send to the viewer is 'Don't come into my painting.' Always add a gap or gate to break the continuity, but not in the centre. In this case, it has been positioned to the left in order to balance the right-hand trees.

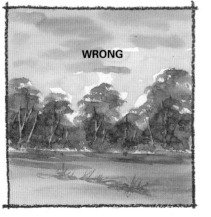

A continuous tree span

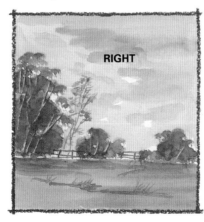

Improved by spaces between trees

3 Continuous tree span

This is similar to above. Vary the height of the trees or bushes and add a few gaps to show a fence. It makes a more pleasing composition. If it isn't feasible to do this, add other features such as sheep or a winding river to direct the eye away from the mass of trees. Alternatively, varying the of colour in the foliage with one or two bright areas will help.

To ensure a pleasing composition, consider your chosen landscape from different viewpoints and select the most inspiring – the best arrangement of the different elements. A successful composition is vital in creating an interesting painting. Always ask yourself basic questions such as: 'What is it that inspires me to paint this scene? Is it the elements in the picture, the effect of light or the atmospheric conditions?' When you have questioned your reasons you may find that the scene doesn't have a focal point. In this case you will need to create one. Use value, counterchange, size, shape, colour, line or direction to create one, but only one: more than one will confuse the viewer. Always try to lead the eye into the painting and out in the distance.

RIGHT AND WRONG POSITIONS (continued)

4 Horizon halfway up the picture

This is a general failing with beginners. It brings back memories of when I began painting. It took time for me to appreciate why other artists' paintings looked so much better than mine. Ideally, place the horizon (in this case, the sea) approximately one third up the painting. Note also that in the left-hand composition, the boat is facing out of the picture, whereas in the right-hand picture, it is facing into the picture.

5 Elements above each other

In the left-hand composition the small building has been placed directly above the larger building. This is not good design – place the buildings diagonally opposite each other instead.

6 Looking directly onto a building

In the left-hand composition the picture is unbalanced. The background mountain is directly above the farmhouse, with the road directed horizontally across the picture and the cloud structure above the mountain. In other words, all of the elements are to the left, leaving little interest on the right.

By taking a viewpoint on the left, the composition is more pleasing. The gable end of the farmhouse can be seen and the elements are more evenly distributed. The track leads the eye into the painting and the darker clouds on the right balance the mountain on the left of the picture.

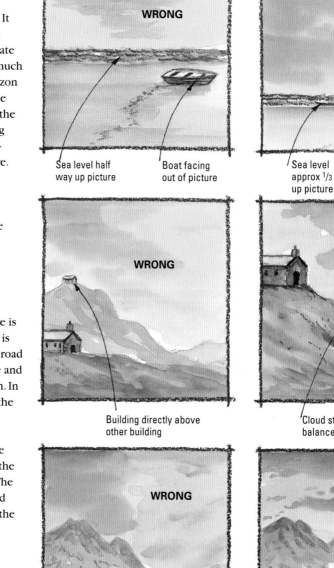
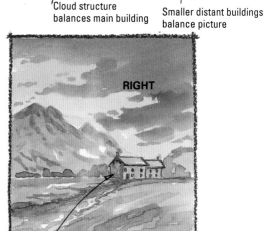

WRONG

RIGHT

Sea level half way up picture | Boat facing out of picture

Sea level approx 1/3 up picture | Boat facing into picture

WRONG

RIGHT

Building directly above other building

Cloud structure balances main building | Smaller distant buildings balance picture

WRONG

RIGHT

Try not to look directly on to building – Show gable end

SUCCESSFUL COMPOSITIONS

To summarise – choose a viewpoint at an angle to the subject, which shows it to its best advantage; simplify, discarding those elements that don't contribute to the success of the painting. Decide what it is about the subject that inspired you to want to paint it and enhance that appeal using value and colour. No matter how inexperienced an artist you think you are, you are different from all other artists, you're unique, because your painting is the equivalent of your handwriting in paint. The following examples are those of compositions that experience has shown are successful. Use them as a guide – there are others that work just as well.

1 The 'L' shape

Here the main elements on the left and across to the right form an 'L' shape. It's important to paint the larger and darker-toned clouds in this example to the right to balance the elements on the left.

2 The double 'L' shape

This composition works if the 'L's are a different height and their bases are on different levels. Paint the foreground 'L' in a darker value than the distant 'L', providing recession in the painting.

3 Compositional balance

Here the main mountain is balanced by the darker clouds. The mountain stream leads the eye into the painting and diagonally balances the mountain.

4 Flowing line

The path leads the eye into and through the painting and out in the distance. This is ideal when painting river scenes or woodland paths.

5 Height and isolation

Very simply painted, a low horizon line and atmospheric sky works well; in this example, one boat on the beach is facing into the picture.

6 Filled area

This is effective for woodland scenes, where the frame is filled with foliage and foreground.

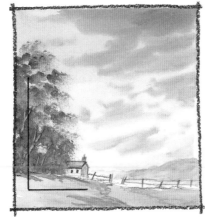

The 'L' shape

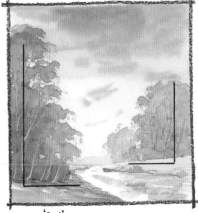

The 'L' double 'L' Shape

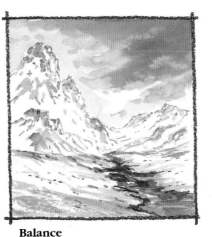

Balance

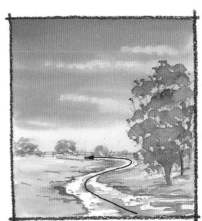

Flowing line

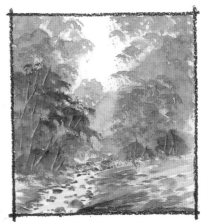

Height and isolation

Filled area

All of the above compositions are pleasing to the eye.

When I'm designing a painting, I think of an expression commonly used in the theatre:

- **Build the set** - the tonal study, the plan.
- **Put in the props** - paint the scene, add the detail.

- **Then light it** - add highlights to make the painting sparkle.

Use your imagination to create the paintings but don't be afraid to break the rules. Enjoy your painting!

WASTWATER – CLOSE UP

In any painting it's important to create recession by painting distant objects in light values and gradually darkening the values as the foreground approaches.

In this painting, I have used tissues folded into wedges, brush strokes and a palette knife to achieve various effects. On page 74 there is a range of techniques for painting mountain structures. You might prefer to study these before coming back to look more closely at this exercise.

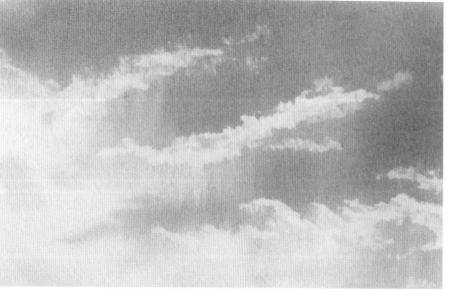

SKY

The traditional wet-in-wet technique has been adopted, whereby the hake brush has been used to apply a pale Raw Sienna wash over the whole of the sky area with a little darker tone applied to selected areas. While this was still wet, stiffer mixes of Payne's Grey/ Cobalt Blue were added to paint the clouds.

A tissue was used to blot out colour to enhance the cloud structures and to soften edges.

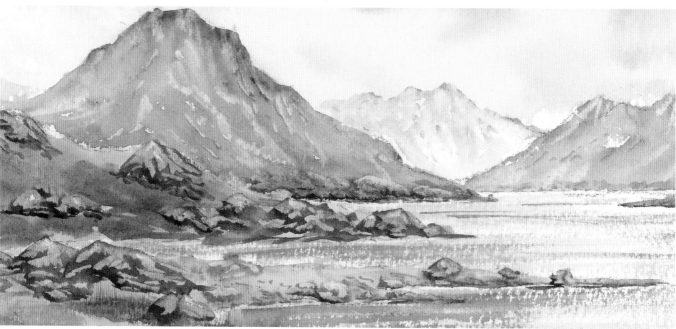

MOUNTAIN AND ROCKS

I have used two brushes to paint the mountains – the 38 mm/1½ in hake to rough out the structure, my brush strokes following the shape of the mountains from peak to ground level and the size 14 round brush to add a variety of colours and detail.

To represent the distant mountains, weak mixes of Cobalt Blue/Alizarin Crimson were used and for those nearer, the foregoing mixes were varied with overpainting using Raw Sienna/Burnt Sienna. Definition was given to the peaks using a Payne's Grey/

Alizarin Crimson mix. The light areas to shape the peaks were achieved by wiping with a tissue shaped to a chisel edge in a downward direction and the rocks were defined using the palette knife (see page 75 for techniques).

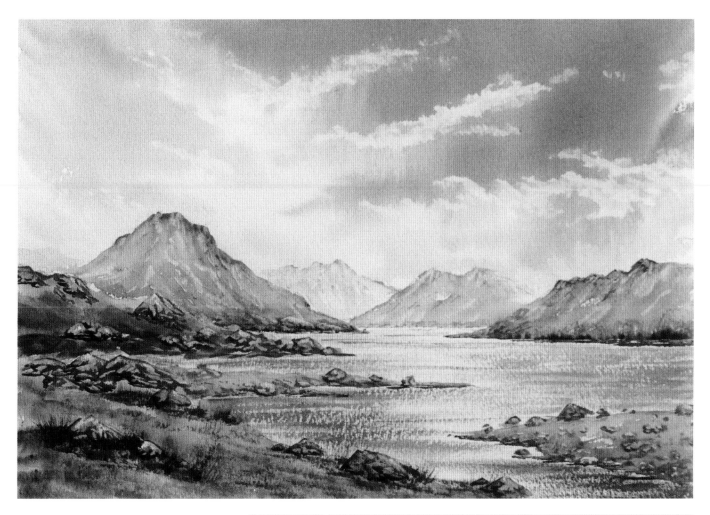

WATER AND FOREGROUND

The foreground was initially completed using mixes of Raw Sienna, with Burnt Sienna added while the underpainting was still wet. By using this technique a more natural effect is achieved. The rocks were painted with the 19 mm/¾ in flat brush and the shapes knifed out using the palette knife.

The foreground grass was painted with the hake brush using various shades of green made from Cobalt Blue/Cadmium Yellow Pale. Finally the water was painted by applying horizontal strokes with the side of the size 14 round brush. The colours were those used for the sky. A light touch of the brush is all that is required to create sparkle on the water.

WHAT YOU WILL NEED.

PAPER:
Saunders Waterford 640 gsm/300 lb Rough

PAINTS:
Payne's Grey, Cobalt Blue, Alizarin Crimson, Raw Sienna, Burnt Sienna, Cadmium Yellow Pale

BRUSHES:
Winsor & Newton Sceptre Gold II Series size 14 round, 19 mm/¾ in flat, 38 mm/1½ in hake

SUPPORTIVE:
Tissues, palette knife

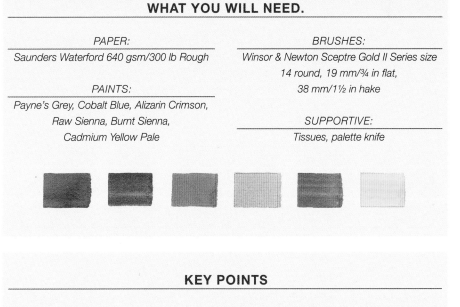

KEY POINTS

1 Paint an atmospheric sky; the darker clouds should be diagonally opposite to balance the larger left-hand mountain.
2 Use the colours in the sky to paint the water to ensure harmony.
3 Use light, quick strokes of the brush to ensure sparkle on the water.
4 Shape the rocks and vary their size and distance apart.

THE POND – PROJECT

This pond makes a lovely composition, but the great variety of colours and tonal values in the foliage need careful thought and planning prior to applying brush to paper.

As always, a quick tonal sketch helps to establish the lights and darks and provides thinking time for planning an approach to the painting. A few quick colour mixes before the start of the painting are helpful in establishing the various greens required.

The painting was completed early in the morning. The distant trees had a blue-green appearance, being shrouded in early morning mist.

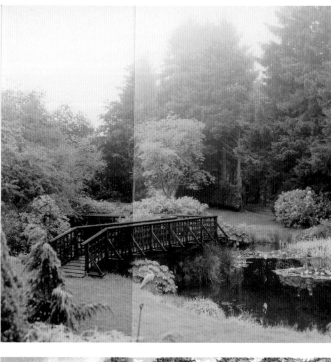

WHAT YOU WILL NEED

PAPER:
Bockingford 425 gsm/200 lb Extra Rough

BRUSHES:
Winsor & Newton Sceptre Gold II size 14 round, size 6 round, size 3 rigger, 19 mm/¾ in flat, 38 mm/1½ in hake, 13 mm/½ in round hog hair brush

COLOURS:
Payne's Grey, Cobalt Blue, Alizarin Crimson, Raw Sienna, Burnt Umber, Cadmium Yellow Pale, Cadmium Yellow Deep, Sap Green

SUPPORTIVE:
Masking fluid, white acrylic paint, dark brown water-soluble crayon

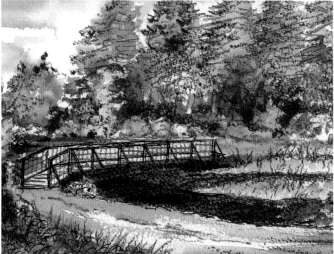

The tonal value study enables you to plan your approach to the painting.

This quick colour representation helps to establish the colour combinations that are needed. I found mixes made from Cadmium Yellow Pale, Raw Sienna, Cobalt Blue and Sap Green were needed for the foliage and mixes of Payne's Grey, Alizarin Crimson and Cobalt Blue for the shadows.

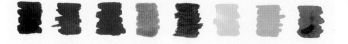

STAGE 1:
DRAWING, MASKING, SKY

An outline drawing was completed using a dark brown water-soluble crayon – only general shapes with little detail, except for the wooden bridge. Masking fluid was used to preserve the structure of the bridge, some trees, branches and the land and grasses on the islands in the pond.

When the masking was dry, a pale wash of Raw Sienna with a little Cobalt Blue was brushed in to paint the misty sky. A 38 mm/1½ in hake was used for this. When dry the distant trees were roughly painted using an old hog hair brush loaded with a pale Cobalt Blue/Raw Sienna mix.

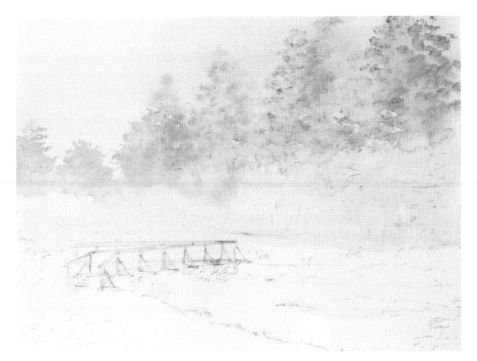

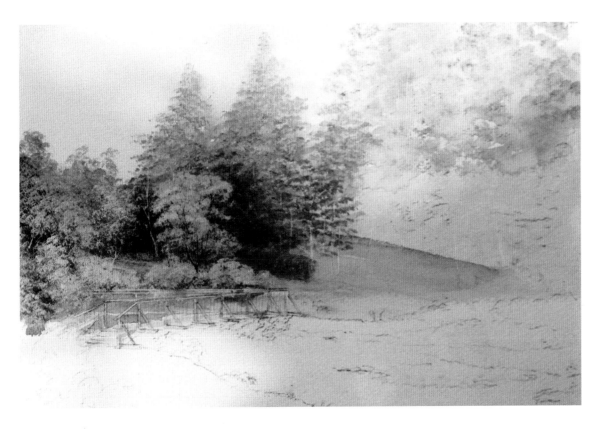

STAGE 2:
TREE FOLIAGE

The left-hand tree/bush groupings were painted using a variety of greens made from Cadmium Yellow Pale, Raw Sienna, Cobalt Blue and Cadmium Yellow Deep. The latter was used for the foreground bush and an old hog hair brush was used to paint the foliage.

The grass area was painted with weak washes of Cadmium Yellow Pale and Cobalt Blue. As can be seen, the masking repelled the paint to indicate tree structures.

When painting such a grouping, it is important to consider it as consisting of a variety of individual trees and bushes displaying different heights and shapes.

The shadows were painted in last, by overpainting areas of foliage with a Payne's Grey/Alizarin Crimson mix, to give depth to the trees.

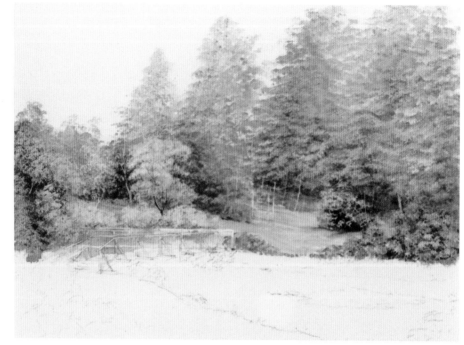

STAGE 3:
TREE GROUPING

The procedure discussed in Stage 2 was followed to complete the tree grouping on the far side of the pond. The colours used were the same. To add a few highlights to the foliage a little white acrylic paint was mixed with the variety of greens. Watercolour white will sink into the paper, so white acrylic or gouache is better, ensuring the paint stays on the surface of the paper, creating light areas that add sparkle to the foliage.

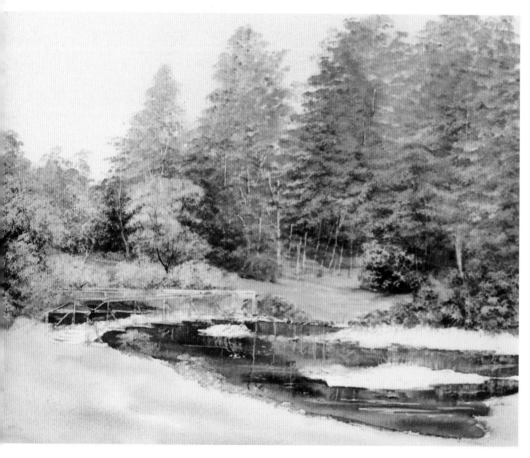

STAGE 4:
FOREGROUND AND WATER

Using the hake, a pale Raw Sienna wash was brushed over the foreground grass. When it was less than one-third dry, darker greens were brushed in, allowing the colours to fuse together, creating a soft effect.

The water was painted using the round brush, loaded initially with a pale Cobalt Blue and while still wet adding dark values using vertical strokes with a Payne's Grey/ Alizarin Crimson mix.

Some green was brushed down to represent reflections. Finally the two small bushes were added. Note how the masking has repelled the paint to indicate tree structures reflecting in the pond.

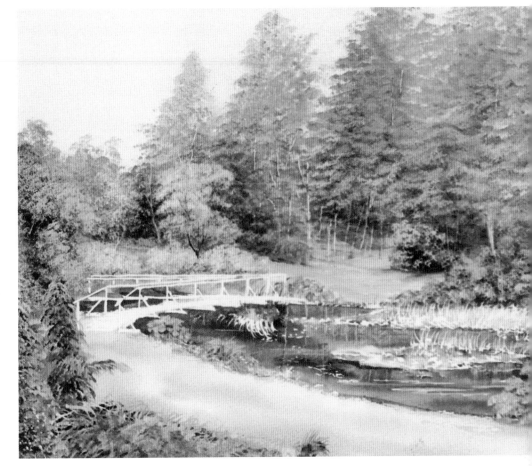

STAGE 5:
THE FOLIAGE

A Raw Sienna wash was applied to the islands in the pond and a little green brushed in here and there. When dry, the masking was removed to reveal the tufts of grass. For this, I always use a putty eraser that adheres to the masking, facilitating removal.

The right-hand bush was painted using previously described techniques. The foreground bushes on the left need to be realistically painted. The green upright conifer and the yellow low-growing bush have lacy branches, which necessitate painting them with a size 3 rigger brush to achieve the right effect.

In both cases the dark background was painted first and when dry a little white acrylic was added to the mixture – for example, Cadmium Yellow Deep for the low growing bush and using quick flicks with the rigger to create the lacy foliage.

Finally, the masking was removed from the bridge.

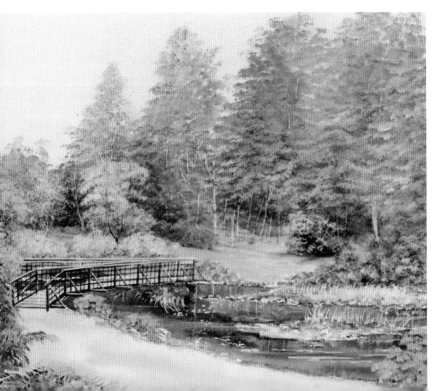

STAGE 6:
BRIDGE

The bridge was painted with a rigger brush using a weak Raw Sienna for the boards and Burnt Umber for the uprights. Light effects were the white of the paper washed over with a very weak Raw Sienna – just a hint of colour.

Raw Sienna washes were applied to the island areas and the grasses under the bridge.

THE POND – PROJECT

KEY POINTS

1 Don't attempt to capture this scene exactly – you can't compete with nature. Just try to convey the essence of the scene that inspired you to paint it.

2 Before putting paint to paper, think through your approach – all paintings need a plan to follow. The tonal study provides you with thinking time and establishes your value patterns.

3 Experiment with mixing a wide range of greens and visualize where they fit into your painting.

4 The bridge over the pond is your focal point. It needs to stand out against its surroundings.

5 Paint each bush and tree freestanding, although part of an overall mass. Those light-toned tree structures are significant. They can be masked as in this project or scratched out with a palette knife, while the paint is less than one-third dry.

6 Don't attempt to complete the painting in one sitting. View it carefully over a few days to establish where a few highlights will improve the painting and where darker values are needed to create depth.

7 A few small details such as shadows in the foreground grass and highlights here and there make all the difference. This is what distinguishes the professional from the amateur.

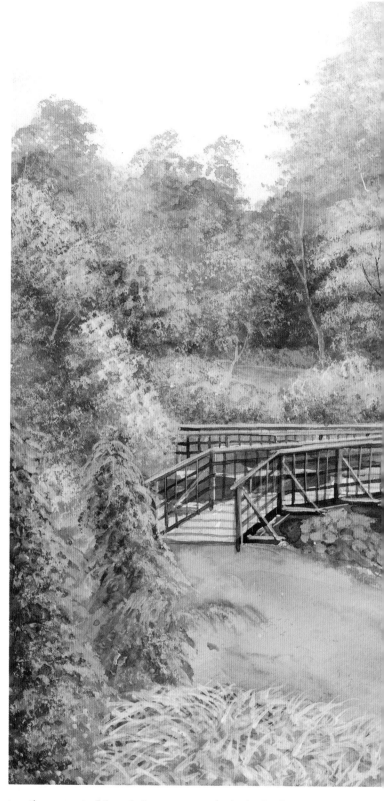

FINAL STAGE:

FINISHING THE PAINTING

The tonal value study is often overlooked by the beginner to landscape painting, yet it is one of the most important stages in the painting process. This monochrome study helps the artist to select the most pleasing composition after viewing the scene from several positions. It allows thinking time prior to applying paint, by estimating the most desirable colours, in this case, for the foliage, which in this composition is quite challenging due to the great variety of shapes, sizes and greens.

Begin by squinting your eyes – by this method the variety of tones and where the shadows are located can best be seen. Identify the focal point area; in this case, the wooden bridge over the pond. This is where the eye is directed when you first look at the scene, so make sure it is distinctive.

The trees and bushes have been painted as individuals but linked together as part of the whole to create unity in the landscape.

I painted this landscape early in the morning in subdued light, yet as an artist I wanted to add some colour to make the painting more pleasing to the viewer. I mixed a Cobalt Blue/Alizarin Crimson colour combination to make a soft purple glaze to apply to the top left area of sky.

Raw Sienna and Cadmium Yellow/Sap Green colours were

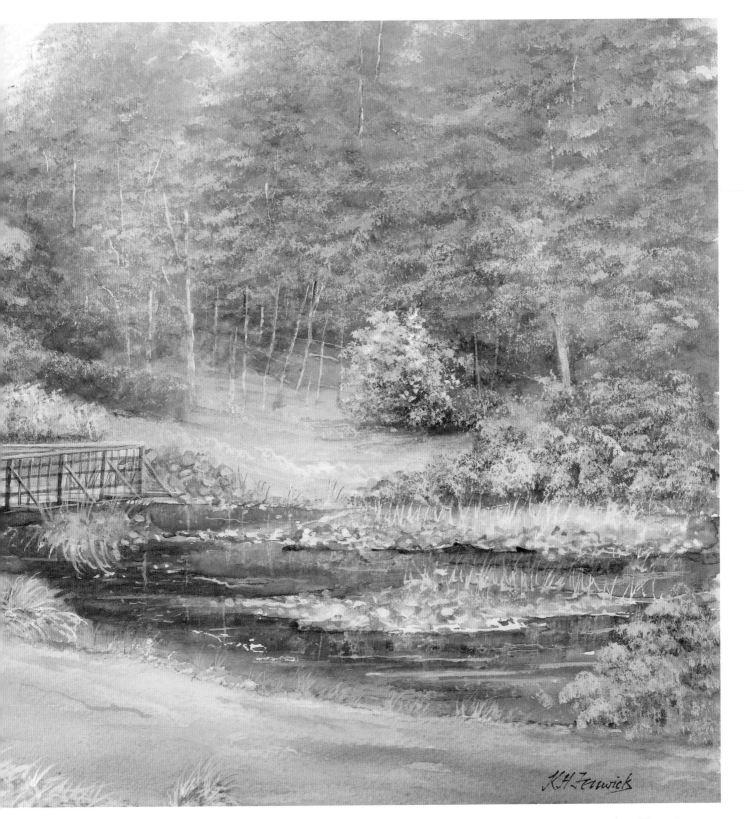

applied to selected shrubs and bushes. These colours were also used to paint the ground cover, and applied wet-in-wet to allow them to mix together to create a fusion of colour.

The pond water required darker values for impact and to separate the land areas and provide contrast with the bridge.

As your painting progresses it is important to stand back and look at the artwork, to establish the most appropriate tonal values. In this painting I made improvements by adding a few tree structures and highlights.

I never complete a painting in one sitting, preferring to look at my composition over several days prior to applying the final brush strokes I feel are necessary. A few carefully placed brush strokes, touches of colour and tonal values can transform an average painting into quality fine art.

THE POND – PROJECT

PAINTING SKIES

The ability to paint a successful sky is important – after all, the sky can represent two-thirds of your painting. They aren't difficult to paint, but there are basic rules that must be followed:

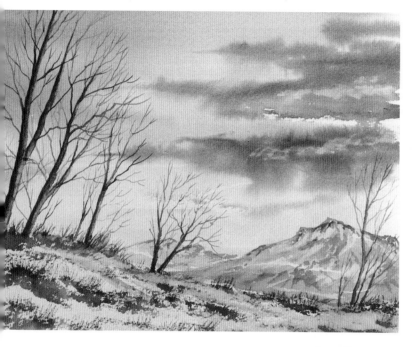

1 Use a large hake brush. I find a 50 mm/2 in brush too large and a 25 mm/1 in brush too small. A 38 mm/1½ in hake is ideal. The hake brush is made of goat hair with the ability to hold a lot of paint, enabling the paper to be covered quickly.

2 When painting cloud structures over a wet underpainting, timing is important. Apply a less wet paint over an underpainting once the shine has left the surface – the underpainting must be less than one-third dry or hard edges will occur.

3 Use a light touch with the brush and apply the minimum number of brush strokes to retain freshness. Just dance across the paper, depositing paint. The sky must be painted in less than three minutes to avoid hard edges.

4 Use an absorbent tissue to control edges and wet runs and to remove paint representing light cloud formations.

In this first example representing an evening sky, a pale Raw Sienna wash was applied overall to the sky area and a little Cobalt Blue added to the top left. The colours blended together. When the underpainting was approximately one-third dry, stiffer mixes of Raw Sienna, Cobalt Blue and Alizarin Crimson were brushed in to represent the evening clouds. A tissue was shaped to a wedge and by using a dabbing action some colour was removed to represent light coloured clouds. Note that I dabbed – not wiped. The stiffer paint will blend in well with the wet underpainting – not a hard edge in sight.

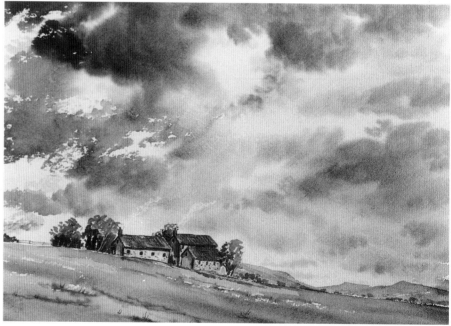

This atmospheric sky was painted by initially applying a Raw Sienna wash approximately two-thirds of the way across the painting, leaving the one-third on the left dry. The 38 mm/1½ in hake brush allowed the paper to be covered quickly. When the underpainting was less than one-third dry, a less wet mix of varying tones of a Cobalt Blue/Alizarin Crimson/Payne's Grey mix was brushed in, using circular movements with the corner of the hake brush to form the cloud structures. The area of dry paper on the left created a different effect to the wet-in-wet washes applied to the right.

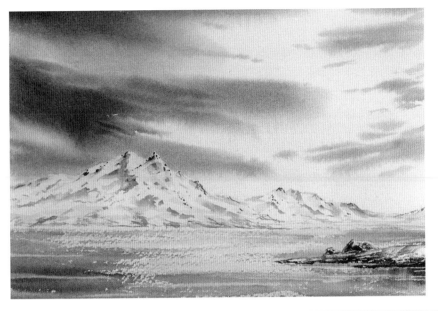

This cirrus sky was painted in less than two minutes by applying a Raw Sienna wash and when the shine had left the surface of the paper, Cobalt Blue cloud structures were painted in. Use broad sweeps of the hake, with an arm, rather than a wrist, movement. When painting skies, the timing is so important to avoid hard edges forming. The result is a lovely fresh sky, without the dreaded hard edges.

For this colourful evening sky, I used the hake brush and a Raw Sienna wash and painted in a little Cadmium Orange. This was followed by Cobalt Blue and even darker clouds made up from a Payne's Grey/Alizarin Crimson mix. The clouds were almost in horizontal layers, painted by simply touching the paper with the edge of the hake brush and allowing the paint to blend with the underpainting. To prevent the cloud layers from running into one large mass, the sky was completed with the paper virtually flat. Finally, a tissue was used to soften the edges and to create a few white clouds. Note the sparkle on the water achieved by using a dry brush effect.

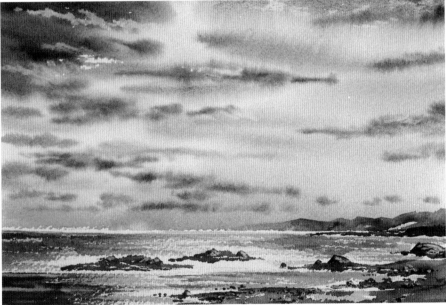

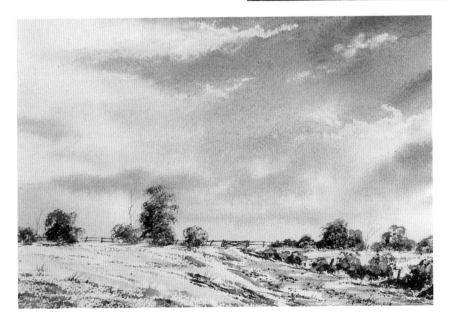

This soft evening sky works well with this landscape. Note that the colours of the sky have been reflected in the foreground snow. Snow is rarely seen as white, as it reflects the colours of the sky and the surrounding elements. The darker cloud elements have been painted on the right to balance the larger bush on the left. Skies are a pleasure to paint. As usual, I have painted a Raw Sienna wash and while still wet, brushed in Alizarin Crimson in some areas, followed by stiffer mixes of Cobalt Blue/Alizarin Crimson.

PAINTING SKIES

SPRINGTIME AT CATHEDRAL ROCKS –
CLOSE UP

Cathedral Rocks in the distance contrast with the flower-filled meadows in Yosemite National Park, which evoke a pastoral scene of peace and tranquillity.

ROCKS

Time was taken to draw the profile of the rocks, ensuring a realistic impression evolved.

The establishment of lights and darks was paramount. Masking fluid was applied to selected areas on the rocks. Initially, the rocks were painted wet-in-wet, with the detail being added when this underpainting was dry. I used Raw Sienna for the underpainting and while still wet, a Payne's Grey/Alizarin Crimson mix was used to paint the shadows to create depth and structure. Cobalt Blue and Burnt Sienna was added to provide variation. Paint one rock at a time – it's like putting together the pieces of a jigsaw. The masking fluid was finally removed using a putty eraser.

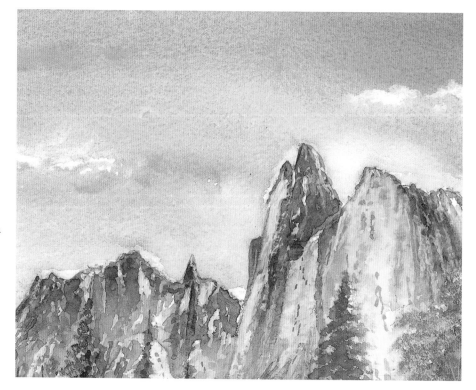

TREES

There are a variety of shapes, sizes and colours displayed in the trees. Although they appear as a total mass across the middle distance, take care to paint each tree with its own identity and don't forget to add the shadows. Trees appear dark on the inside and lighter on the outside. Add a few highlights to create sparkle. The techniques for painting trees are shown on pages 96–99.

MEADOW

Using the hake brush, a pale Raw Sienna with a little Sap Green was painted in the distance with more Sap Green being added as the foreground is approached; for the darker shadows some Payne's Grey was

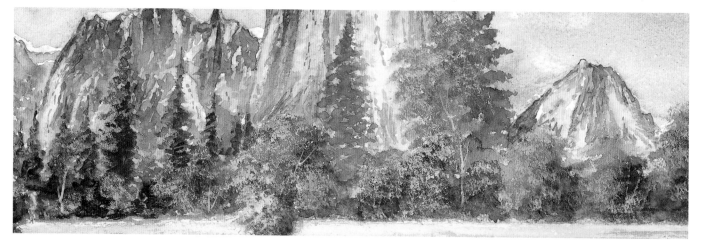

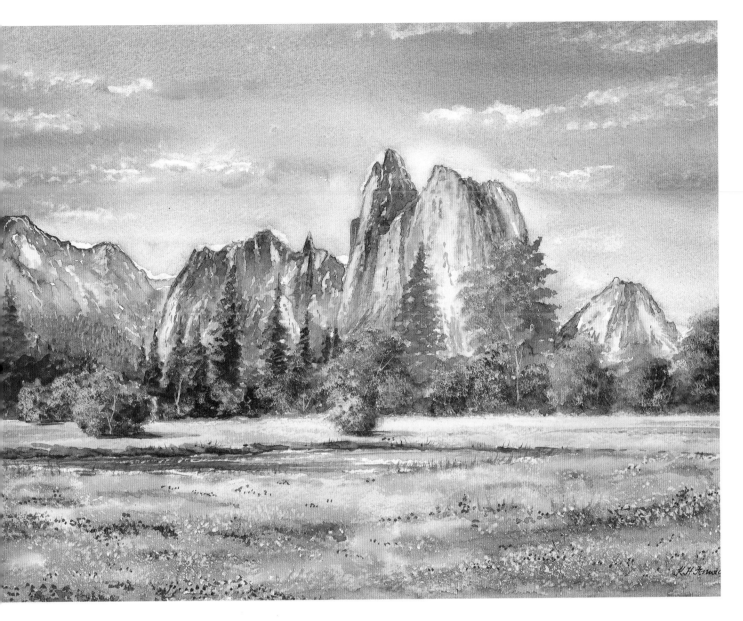

added to the mix. When dry, the flowers were added using two different techniques: a stippling action with the hog hair brush, and spattering colour by running a thumb over the bristles of an old toothbrush to control the direction of spatter. When spattering, it is important to mask above the horizon line, or the spatter will spray everywhere. An ordinary piece of newspaper is fine for this purpose.

KEY POINTS

1 Produce a tonal study to establish the lights and darks, in particular, to add to depth and form the rocks.
2 Paint a simple sky, in this case, Cobalt Blue with white clouds created by removing paint with a tissue.
3 Paint your trees as individual shapes.
4 Create variation in the foreground by applying several values.
5 Use old newspaper to mask areas of the painting prior to spattering.
6 For unity, add touches of the foreground colours to the rocks and trees.

WHAT YOU WILL NEED

PAPER:
Saunders Waterford 640 gsm/300 lb Rough

BRUSHES:
Winsor & Newton Sceptre Gold II Series 19 mm/¾ in flat, size 3 rigger, 38 mm/1½ in hake, 19 mm/¾ in round bristle

COLOURS:
Payne's Grey, Cobalt Blue, Alizarin Crimson, Raw Sienna, Burnt Sienna, Cadmium Yellow Pale, Sap Green

SUPPORTIVE:
Masking fluid, old toothbrush

SPRINGTIME AT CATHEDRAL ROCKS

COLOUR MIXING
– USEFUL COLOUR COMBINATIONS

Most beginners in watercolour painting experience difficulty in mixing colours. Some of my students go to extremes. They have been told that all they will need is three primary colours, consisting of a red, yellow and blue, and from these they will be able to mix any colours they require; others arrive with dozens of different colours, including horrendous turquoise blues and garish greens and a variety of greys.

Colour has fascinated artists for generations. Many books have been written about this subject but there's no substitute for experience. I'm often asked by my students the percentages of each hue I have mixed together to achieve a particular colour but I can't really tell them – I just mix quantities of colour together until I am satisfied with the outcome. Certain rules obviously have to be followed. If fresh, clean colours are required, it's best to mix only two colours but for more subtle shades, mix three colours together. If more than three colours are mixed, they are likely to produce dull colours which artists call 'mud', but there may be occasions when a dull colour is needed.

THE BASICS OF COLOUR MIXING

The PRIMARY colours are: RED, YELLOW and BLUE. If similar quantities of each primary colour are mixed together, the result is almost a black colour, as shown in the colour circle below. If blue and yellow are mixed together they will produce green; mixing red and yellow gives an orange, and red and blue produces a violet or purple colour. These are known as SECONDARY colours. If a primary colour is mixed with a secondary colour, TERTIARY colours are created.

Follow the arrows in the colour circle below – it's easy. By using three primary colours in the combination shown with various amounts of water, a wide range of tints can be produced but of course, companies such as Winsor & Newton produce over 90 colours, allowing plenty of scope to experiment.

For your first exercise, follow the arrows in the colour circle. The colours and tints you will produce will depend on which particular red, yellow and blue you mix and the amount of water you add. For the exercises in this section, I suggest you purchase a small watercolour pad and experiment to build yourself a colour mixing resource to which you can refer as required, until mixing becomes second nature. Don't forget to record your mixing combinations.

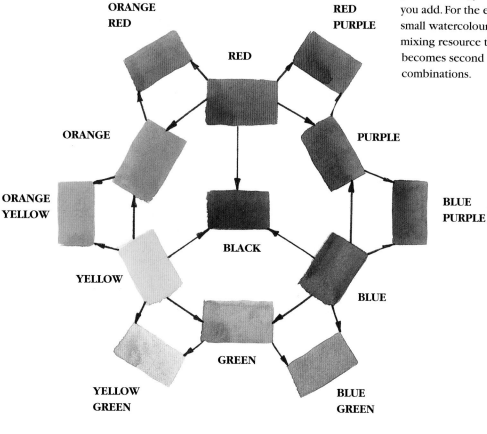

ORANGE RED   RED   RED PURPLE

ORANGE   PURPLE

ORANGE YELLOW   BLACK   BLUE PURPLE

YELLOW   BLUE

YELLOW GREEN   GREEN   BLUE GREEN

By varying the amount of each colour and water content, various shades and tones can be mixed.

Common sense tells you that if you wish to mix a light tone, you should start with the lighter colour and add a small amount of the darker colour. If you're aiming to mix a dark colour, start with the dark colour and add a small amount of the lighter colour until you achieve the required tone.

For example, if you require a rich orange red, then start with the red and add a small amount of yellow. For a bright orange, start with yellow and add a small amount of red. To lighten your colours, add more clean water. A useful exercise for you to try is to mix two colours together using a little water to achieve a dark tone and paint a small area on a sheet of watercolour paper. Hold some absorbent tissue (toilet roll) in your hand, dip the paint-loaded brush without shaking or wiggling it into the water pot to a depth of about 1 cm/½ in, then remove it gently, wipe it on the tissue and make an adjoining deposit on the paper. You will observe your colour mix has become lighter in tone. Repeat this process (without dipping the brush into your original colour mix) and you will be able to produce between six and twelve tones of the original colour. Practising this will give you confidence in colour mixing and your painting skills will improve faster.

When mixing colours, never dip your brush into the middle of the paint. I always tease the paint away, using circular movements of the brush, lightly touching the side of the deposited paint. By this means, I'm able to control the strength of paint on the brush and it helps to keep my wrist supple.

My preference is to use tube colours, as the paint is soft and responsive. I prefer to mix two colours together, sometimes three to create a particular colour. If more than three colours are mixed together, the likelihood of creating a dull colour, often referred to as 'mud' is almost certain.

I use my supportive palette and any other colours that I feel I require for special effects but in the main, 90% of my paintings are completed from my basic palette.

Below left, I have shown how I lay out my colours on the palette. They are laid out to a system, starting with Payne's Grey. Clockwise, the first three are my sky colours, the next three, my earth colours and the following two my mixers.

I cover my palette with plastic wrap prior to depositing paint, which enables me to clean the palette with ease, using a soft tissue. When it becomes too messy to clean easily, I simply remove the wrap and start again. This saves me the task of having to clean my palette under the tap.

MY BASIC PALETTE

Most of my paintings are made with the following colours in tube form:

Payne's Grey	Cerulean Blue	Alizarin Crimson
Raw Sienna	Burnt Sienna	Burnt Umber
Cadmium Yellow Pale	Permanent Sap Green	

MY SUPPORTIVE PALETTE

Sometimes I use these extra colours to complement my basic palette as required:

French Ultramarine	Cobalt Blue	Winsor Yellow
Gold Ochre	Brown Madder	Vermilion hue
Cadmium Orange	Winsor Red	

By positioning the paint deposits around the perimeter of the palette, I am able to draw the colours into its centre to mix my required colour. The larger your mixing area, the less restricted you are. Those tiny palettes with small indentations don't allow the use of large brushes and don't provide adequate mixing areas. I use my 38 mm/1½ in sky and texture brush (hake) for most of my painting, but it is unusable in the indentations provided in a small palette.

THE SECRETS OF WATERCOLOUR PAINTING

1. Use the largest brushes possible in relation to the size of the element you're painting to ensure freshness.
2. Use the minimum number of brush strokes.
3. Use a light touch of the brush loaded with fresh colour over the surface of a rough paper to create texture.
4. Success with watercolour painting comes with knowing how wet the paint on the brush is in relation to the wetness or dryness of the paper and when to apply the paint.
5. To avoid hard edges forming, each successive layer of paint should be drier than the underpainting. Once the underpainting becomes more than one-third dry, hard edges will occur if you apply wet paint.

SOME COLOUR COMBINATIONS THAT I FIND USEFUL

Practise mixing the colours here and those on pages 62-65 until they become second nature.

PAINTING SKIES

MIXING BLUES:

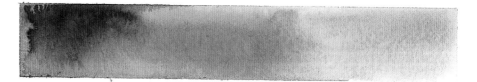

Payne's Grey/Cerulean Blue - cloud colours

Payne's Grey/French Ultramarine - cloud colours

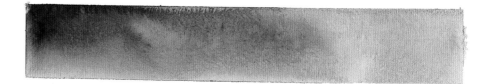

Payne's Grey/Alizarin Crimson - warm cloud colours

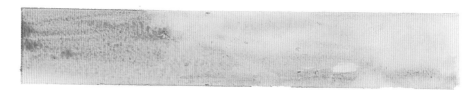

Raw Sienna - underpainting

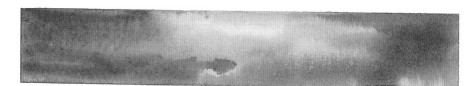

Cobalt Blue or Indanthrene Blue - deep blue clouds

COLOUR HARMONY

One of the best ways to ensure colour harmony in a painting is to use a limited range of colours. For example, the sky could be painted blue, the mountains a blue green, the water blue and the foreground bank and trees green. Using only three colours – Cerulean Blue, Cadmium Yellow and Payne's Grey, plus various amounts of water – enables you to paint a wide range of spring and summer scenes.

Similarly, by using mixes of Raw Sienna, Burnt Sienna and French Ultramarine, autumn scenes can be created.

PAINTING TREES AND BUSHES

MIXING GREENS:

Payne's Grey/Sap Green – dark rich greens

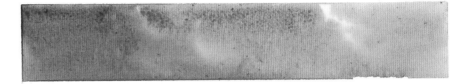

Sap Green/Raw Sienna – yellow greens

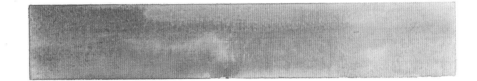

Cerulean Blue/Cadmium Yellow Pale – spring greens

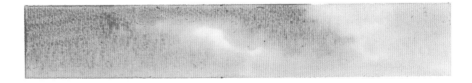

Cerulean Blue/Raw Sienna – olive greens

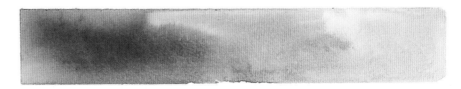

Payne's Grey/Cadmium Yellow Pale – mid grass green

French Ultramarine/Winsor Yellow – bright greens

COLOUR MIXING

MIXING AUTUMN FOLIAGE

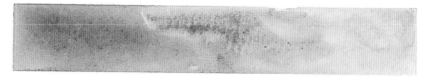

Burnt Sienna/Raw Sienna – warm browns

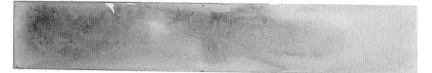

Alizarin Crimson/Raw Sienna – rich reds/oranges

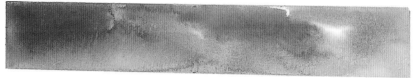

Alizarin Crimson/Cadmium Yellow Pale – warm oranges

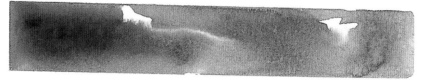

Payne's Grey/Alizarin Crimson – purple grey

MIXING GREYS

Twenty per cent of any colour on your palette mixed with 80 per cent Payne's Grey will result in an extensive range of cool and warm greys. My favourites are those shown right:

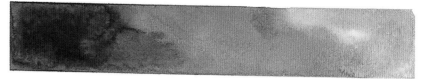

Payne's Grey/Sap Green – dark rich green grey

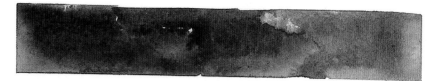

Payne's Grey/Burnt Sienna – dark brown grey

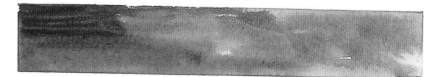

Payne's Grey/Cerulean Blue – depth in distant trees

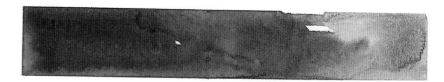

French Ultramarine/Alizarin Crimson – warm shadow grey

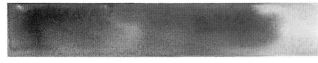

Payne's Grey/Sap Green - dark water under trees

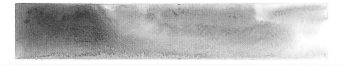

Payne's Grey/Cerulean Blue - surface water

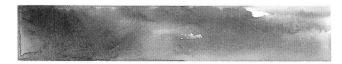

Payne's Grey/French Ultramarine - bright surface water

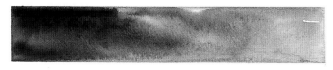

Payne's Grey/Alizarin Crimson - pale shadows

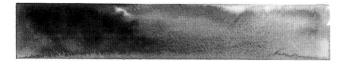

Payne's Grey/Burnt Umber - dark shadows

Don't forget that water is colourless but its surface reflects the sky colours and those of surrounding objects. For colour harmony in your painting the colour of the water should reflect the sky colours.

PAINTING MOUNTAINS

Raw Sienna/Sap Green - trees and grassy areas

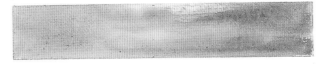

Raw Sienna/Burnt Sienna - underpainting

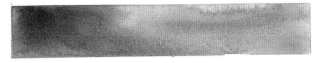

Payne's Grey/Alizarin Crimson - mountain peaks and shadows

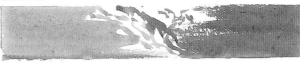

Cerulean Blue or Cobalt Blue - shadows

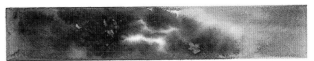

Payne's Grey/Burnt Umber - dark promontories

PAINTING ROCKS

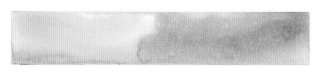

Raw Sienna/Burnt Sienna - warmth

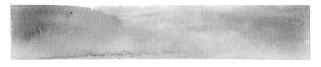

Payne's Grey/Cerulean Blue - cold underpainting

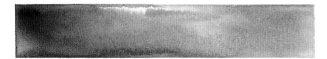

Payne's Grey/Alizarin Crimson - warm shadows

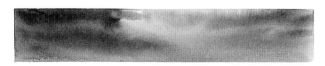

Payne's Grey/Burnt Umber - dark shadows/texture

Davy's Gray or Raw Sienna - underpainting

PAINTING BUILDINGS

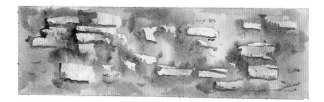

Raw Sienna - underpainting
Burnt Sienna - variation in texture
Burnt Umber - darker texture/cracks/crevices/weathering

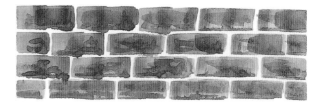

Payne's Grey/Alizarin Crimson - cracks/crevices/weathering
Cobalt Blue/Alizarin Crimson - shadows/weathered effects
Vermilion/Alizarin Crimson - brick colour

PAINTING STONE WALLS AND BRIDGES

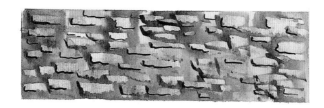

Raw Sienna or neutral grey - underpainting
Burnt Umber - variation
French Ultramarine/Alizarin Crimson - shadows/texture
Payne's Grey/Alizarin Crimson - dark shadows, depth
Burnt Sienna/Burnt Umber - dark texture

Raw Sienna - underpainting for sky

Cobalt Blue - snow shadows

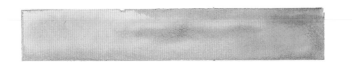

Raw Sienna/Alizarin Crimson - underpainting for evening sky

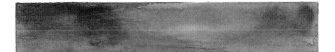

Payne's Grey/Alizarin Crimson - cloud colours for evening sky

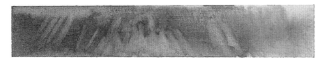

Payne's Grey/Cerulean Blue - rain clouds

Payne's Grey/Raw Sienna - rain clouds/mist/fog

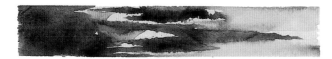

Payne's Grey/Burnt Umber - storm clouds

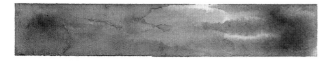

Payne's Grey/Burnt Umber/Alizarin Crimson - storm clouds

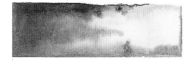

French Ultramarine over Cadmium Yellow Pale - light in the sky

Mixing greens and greys - mentioned earlier in text

PUDDLE PAINTING

A technique often used by the professional artist to achieve colour harmony is to mix a range of coloured washes on the palette and as colour mixing progresses, the brush is dipped into these mixes to create similar base colours throughout the painting, avoiding extremes of colours.

Painting should be fun and experimenting with colours is no exception. You will be amazed at the range of colours and shades that can be achieved. Above all else, enjoy your painting.

PAINTING WATER

Water is a challenging and exciting subject for the watercolourist. There's nothing that helps to establish the effect of peace and tranquillity like painting near a stretch of water, particularly moving water as it splashes off protruding rocks. It engenders a sense of well-being that inspires the artist to produce their best work.

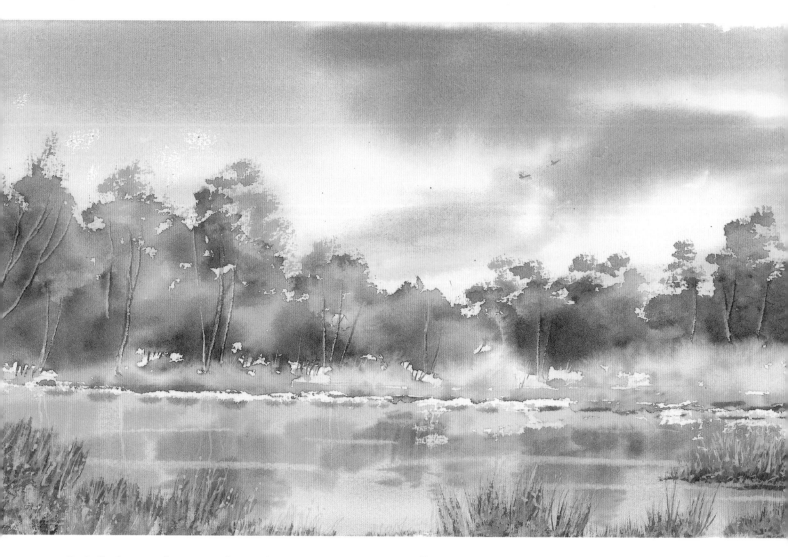

Basically, there are three types of water the artist needs to represent:

MOTIONLESS – a still lake, a pond or even a puddle in a country lane is included in this category;

MOVING – consider a slow-flowing river, a windswept lake or a mountain beck;

TURBULENT – includes a turbulent seascape, a fast-flowing river or a mountain stream cascading over a rocky base or a waterfall.

Representing water in a painting needs an understanding of the techniques necessary and the most suitable brushes to be used to enable the artist to illustrate effectively the type of water required.

The colours will vary, depending on the source of water and the land over which it flows. For example, if the land is peaty, the water may have Burnt Sienna tinges, but if the water bed is rocky, the water may be perfectly clear and its surface will show the cloud colours and reflections of adjacent objects. For water to look real it should be painted with minimum brush strokes. There are many examples in this book enabling you to study and practise your new-found techniques.

SPRING

REFLECTIONS

Water in reality is colourless; its surface colour reflects the colour of the sky and that of reflecting objects in general. However, if the water is flowing over land rich in mineral deposits, then it may be coloured by those.

The sharpness of reflections will depend on the speed of flow. If water is flowing quickly, the reflections will appear blurred; if the water is motionless the reflections will appear as a mirror image. There only has to be a slight wind blowing across the surface and the areas of light and dark can change significantly. When painting water, don't attempt to change it every time the surface colours and values change. Keep a picture in your mind and paint it as you remember it in the first place.

The simplest way to paint reflections is to paint an initial wash, (usually the colours in the sky) and, using a 19 mm/¾ in flat brush, pull down vertical strokes of the colours in the reflecting objects – in the painting opposite, it is the trees. Notice a few wind lines have been created by wiping a tissue folded to the shape of a chisel edge across the paper to remove paint.

BRUSH STROKES

The following exercises cover virtually all of the techniques you will need to paint water effectively. Practise these techniques; they will serve you well.

1 SPARKLE ON WATER

Think of your paper surface as mountains and valleys. Move the side of the size 14 round brush loaded with moist paint, quickly and lightly over the peaks of the paper. The valleys (white of the paper) will be left uncovered, creating a

broken wash, ideal for representing sparkles on water. See page 47.

2 WATERFALLS

Use the 38 mm/1½ in hake brush to create the effect of falling water. Make a quick circular motion, lightly touching the paper to deposit paint. The action is just a quick twitch of the brush. Practise the technique on a similar piece of paper until the paint is being deposited to your satisfaction before applying it to your painting. Build up gradually, applying at least two tonal values, working from light to dark. See pages 73, 79.

3 FAST-FLOWING WATER

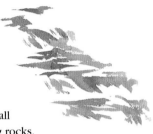

This is the technique that I use when painting a fast-flowing river or mountain stream. Using the hake brush, I touch the paper to deposit paint and in between deposits, I twitch the brush to represent small falls of water between protruding rocks. The whole action is completed in seconds; a dab followed by a twitch repeated, working from the distance to the foreground.

4 WAVES

Apply curved motions with the hake brush to create the effects of waves. Work light to dark, leaving some white paper

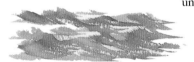

uncovered. Build up the values stage by stage. Stand back and observe; don't rush it. See page 68.

5 DISTANT SEASCAPE

To produce a believable impression of distant waves, use the full width of the hake to deposit paint. The action is to touch the paper, depositing a 38 mm/1½ in line of paint, progressing along the line to the end. Paint each line this way and then use the corner of the hake to twitch the brush, spreading the deposited line slightly to represent breaking waves.

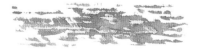

SEASCAPE – CLOSE UP

This is an exercise to demonstrate the use of the brush stroke shown on page 67. The tonal study establishes the value patterns acting as the route plan for the painting. All paintings need a plan. The few minutes needed to produce these simple, monochrome 'doodles' using a water-soluble crayon is time well spent.

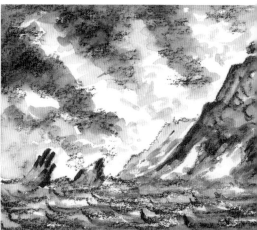

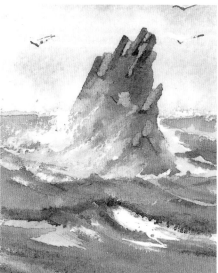

SKY

I wanted an atmospheric sky to balance the rough surface of the sea. A Cerulean Blue wash was over-painted while less than one-third dry using a Payne's Grey/Alizarin Crimson mix to represent cloud structures. Note the diagonal direction of the clouds, helping to create a sense of wind and movement.

ROCKS

The two smaller rocks have been painted to improve the composition by helping to balance the cliff face. Their profile is jagged and directed towards the cliff face, which tends to lead the eye into the painting. Washes were applied and the light areas created by moving paint with a palette knife – see page 75. The effect of waves splashing against the rocks was achieved by flicking upwards with the moist white water-soluble crayon.

WATER

Using the technique for painting waves shown on page 67, the sea was quickly painted. Curved strokes with the hake, reflecting the shape of the waves, can create a realistic effect. Start by applying the lighter tones, followed by darker tones of the same mix. I used mixes of Cerulean Blue for the underpainting, followed by darker tones of a Cerulean Blue/Sap Green/ Payne's Grey mix.

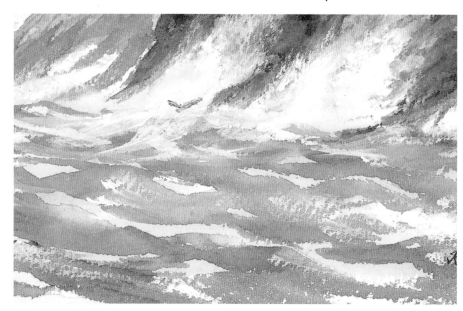

SPRING

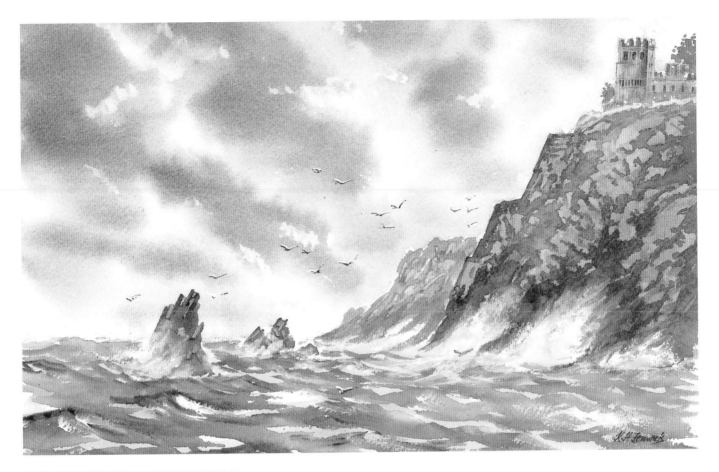

WHAT YOU WILL NEED

PAPER:
Bockingford 425 gsm/200 lb Extra Rough

BRUSHES:
Winsor & Newton Sceptre Gold II Series
19 mm/¾ in flat, size 3 rigger and
38 mm/1½ in hake

COLOURS:
Payne's Grey, Cerulean Blue, Alizarin Crimson,
Raw Sienna, Burnt Sienna, Sap Green

SUPPORTIVE:
White water-soluble crayon, tissue
or kitchen roll

CLIFF FACE

Beginning with a wash of Raw Sienna, brush in Burnt Sienna and a Payne's Grey/Alizarin Crimson mix for dark tones. When the paint is about one-third dry, use the palette knife to create the structure. With a moist tissue, wipe upwards to remove paint, representing waves on the cliff face.

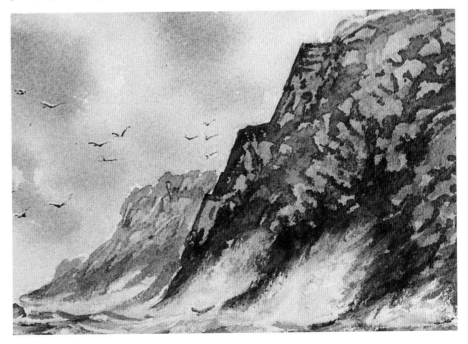

Fast Flow is a painting created from my imagination. It is the type of landscape that stirs my emotions as an artist. Although it's not an actual scene, each of the elements represents features that I have seen previously. I have merely linked them together like a jigsaw to create a painting, taking into consideration the principles of good design.

Although a novice artist may look at a painting like this with apprehension, thinking of it in terms of the different elements will make it more manageable. The important thing is not to be deterred from experimenting with it.

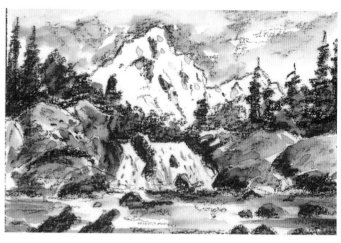

TONAL STUDY

A simple tonal study produced with a water-soluble crayon helps me to establish the composition and values. It ensures that I have thought through my approach to the painting before applying brush to paper. All paintings must have a plan to follow.

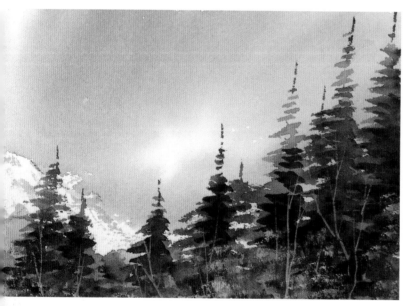

SKY AND FIR TREES

Remember the golden rule when painting skies; if the foreground is detailed, the sky should be simply painted. With this in mind, the sky was painted by washing a very pale Raw Sienna wash over the area and using the 38 mm/1½ in hake loaded with Cobalt Blue. Some cloud structures were painted as soon as the shine had gone off the underpainting.

The fir trees were painted after the mountain and sky area was dry, using the full width of a 19 mm/¾ in flat brush loaded with a Burnt Sienna/Sap Green mix. Start at the base and work upwards, gradually decreasing the amount of the brush face in contact with the paper to produce the desired shape.

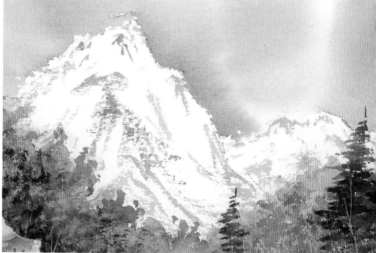

MOUNTAINS

I wanted to keep the mountains simple and pale in tone with little detail to ensure recession in the painting. Prior to painting the sky, it's a good idea to paint masking fluid around the perimeter of the mountain to ensure the paint doesn't run over the white of the paper to be preserved for the mountains when painting the snow. When the sky is dry, remove the masking.

To create the impression of a few promontories projecting through the snow, the dry brush technique was adopted, using the side of the size 6 round brush loaded with Cobalt Blue.

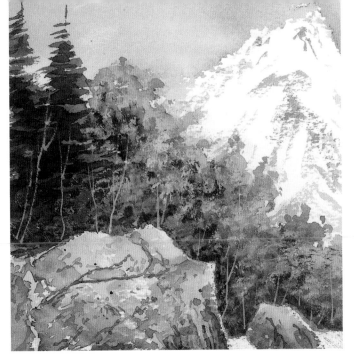

AUTUMN TREES

To paint the autumn trees, variation was achieved by mixing Cadmium Yellow Pale, Raw Sienna, Burnt Sienna and Payne's Grey with a little Sap Green being brushed in here and there.

When the paint was approximately one-third dry, some tree structures were scratched in with the corner of a palette knife.

ROCKS

The rocks are a main feature in this painting, with more detail being added to the larger rock to the left of the fall.

When painting rocks, I use many techniques available to me. This feature rock was painted as follows. Having initially drawn the shapes with a dark brown water-soluble crayon, a wash of Raw Sienna was painted over the rock as a whole. While still wet, some Burnt Sienna and Burnt Sienna/Payne's Grey was brushed in, using the 19 mm/¾ in flat. An absorbent paper tissue was used to blot chosen areas, creating light effects, and when the paint was approximately one-third dry a palette knife was used to move the paint, creating various rock-like patterns. When that was dry, a rigger brush loaded with darker tones was used to paint shadow and fissures in the rocks.

When all the paint had dried, using an old toothbrush loaded with a Payne's Grey/Burnt Sienna mix, I spattered paint over the rock after masking it with paper off-cuts placed around its profile.

WHAT YOU WILL NEED

PAPER:
640 gsm/300 lb Saunders Waterford Rough

BRUSHES:
Winsor & Newton Sceptre Gold II Series size 14 round, size 6 round, size 3 rigger, 19 mm/¾ in flat, 38 mm/1½ in hake

COLOURS:
Payne's Grey, Cobalt Blue, Raw Sienna, Burnt Sienna, Cadmium Yellow Pale, Sap Green

SUPPORTING:
Dark brown and white water-soluble crayons, masking fluid, paper tissues

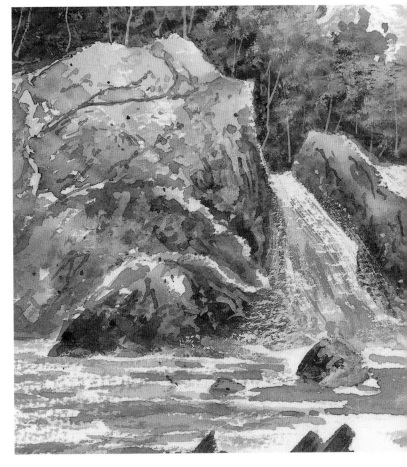

FAST FLOW – CLOSE UP

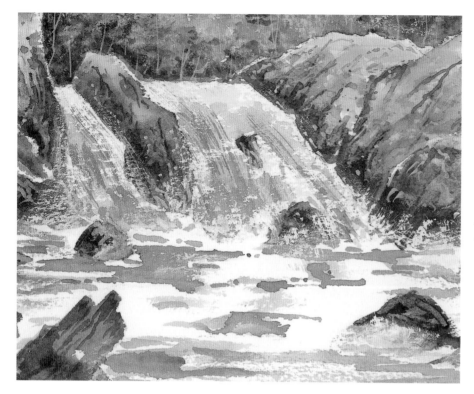

LEVEL WATER

Because the fall of water is flowing fast, there will be lots of white water in the foreground. It's important therefore to leave plenty of the white of the paper uncovered.

To complete the water, I have used the hake brush loaded with a Payne's Grey/Cobalt Blue mix and simply danced quickly across the paper, depositing the paint, taking care not to overdo it.

You will note that I have painted two foreground rocks more jagged than the surrounding rocks to provide variation.

WATERFALL

This is the most tricky part of the painting as overworking can spoil the whole effect. Before applying paint to your painting, practise the brush strokes shown on page 67 on an off-cut of a similar type of watercolour paper to determine the amount of paint needed to produce the desired effect. Don't be in a hurry; think it through first. Begin with a weak Cobalt Blue to establish the main flow patterns. A quick downward twitch of the hake is all that is needed – don't overdo it. Let the paint dry and lightly twitch again with a darker tone, made by adding a little Payne's Grey to the Cobalt Blue. Less is more, when painting a fall of water.

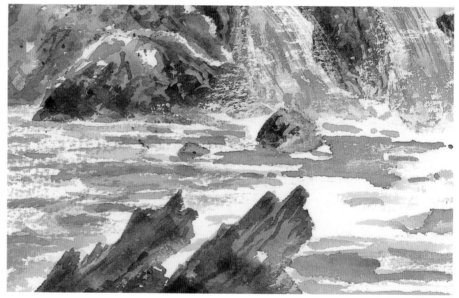

KEY POINTS

1 The sky and mountains need to be simply painted in pale values to achieve recession.
2 Build up the painting of the water gradually, having a pause for thought. Remember that less is more.
3 Use masking fluid to profile your mountains. It will prevent the sky colours running down over the white of the paper.

4 Make the left-hand rock group a feature and use the darker-toned trees behind them to create counterchange.
5 Leave the white of the paper to represent white water.
6 Use a palette knife to create tree structure and to shape the rocks.

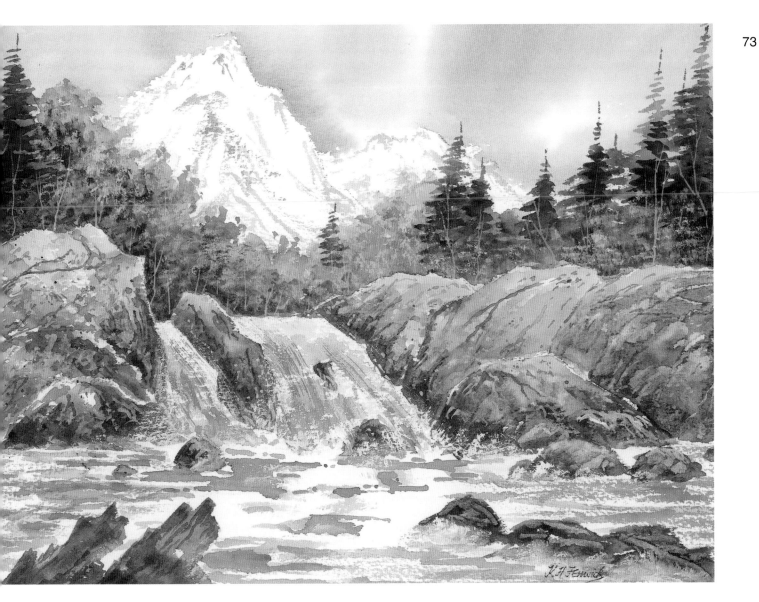

THE COMPLETED PAINTING

Bringing the painting together is an important stage. I normally prefer to critically examine all aspects of the painting spread over a few days before making the final changes that are usually required. The painting must appear as a unit when finished. With a little Burnt Sienna on a size 6 brush, I added colour to the different elements throughout the painting. Using a softened white water-soluble crayon, I deposited paint to represent splashes back over the rocks by flicking upwards from the waterline. This is a useful technique. Similarly, in the case of the rocks shown below, the softened water-soluble crayon can provide the effect I want. Note how the water reflects the sky colours and how the colour combinations used for the rocks are echoed throughout the painting. This is important to achieve unity in a painting.

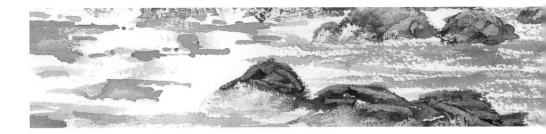

FAST FLOW – CLOSE UP

PAINTING MOUNTAINS AND ROCKS

There are always several different approaches to painting landscapes, including mountains or rocks. The techniques chosen will really depend on the structure of the mountain observed or the atmospheric aspect at the time. For example, in fog or mist, little detail can be seen and the answer may be simple washes to achieve the desired result. On a sunny day with light highlighting specific features, one's approach will be different, with more detail being painted, while when rain falls the colours take on a different aspect. Some of the techniques I use are shown below.

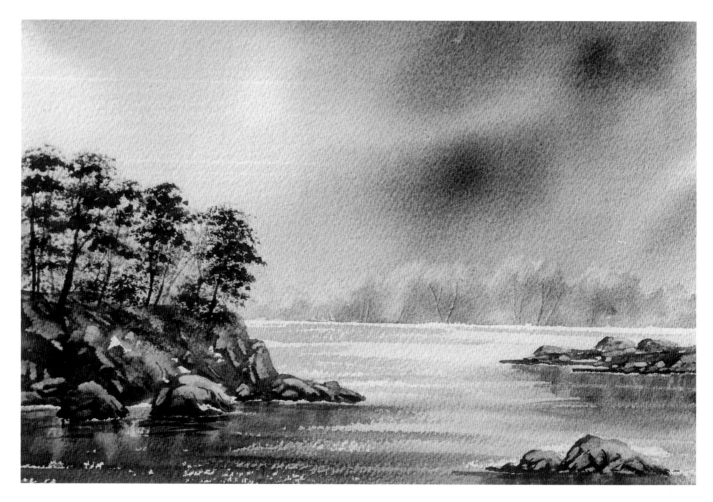

The rocks in this quick sketch were developed effectively by moving paint with the side of a palette knife to create their structure.

WASHES AND TISSUE

The mountains shown below were painted using a 38 mm/1½ in hake brush and applying various washes from peak to ground level, following the structure of the mountain. While the paint was still wet, a tissue was folded into a wedge. Working from the peaks downward the wedge was used to wipe off paint to create highlights and give the impression of structure.

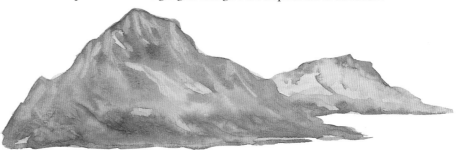

WET-IN-WET

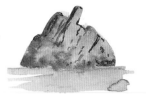

Here I have applied a Raw Sienna wash and dropped in a little Burnt Sienna, allowing the colours to blend together to create a warm underpainting. This was followed by darker tonal values being added with a little Burnt Umber brushed in. When that was dry, I added further detail.

When painting rocks it is important to use colours that are as near to nature as possible. I could have used Davy's Grey and added a Payne's Grey/Alizarin Crimson mix. Rock colour depends on the region but the technique is the same.

WET-IN-WET AND PALETTE KNIFE

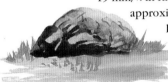

This rock was painted by applying the usual washes with a 19 mm/¾ in flat brush and when they were approximately one-third dry, using a palette knife to move the paint to achieve a realistic look. Practise this technique; you will be amazed how easy it is.

PALETTE KNIFE

The crags below were painted by initially applying several different-coloured washes with a 19 mm/¾ in flat brush and when they were about one-third dry using the side or point of the palette knife to move the paint to produce the desired effect. How much side of the knife you press to the paper will depend on how narrow or wide you wish the finished marks to appear. This 'doodle' was painted in less than two minutes.

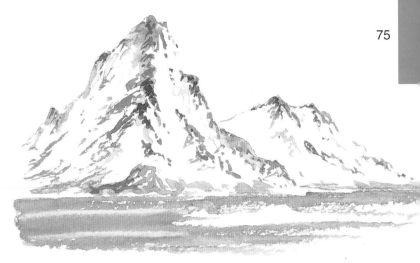

SNOW-CAPPED

Painting snow-capped mountains requires a little finesse and patience as they can so easily be overdone. There are several examples in this book. The white of the paper represents the snow. A Cerulean Blue wash represents the shadows and the darker tones of a Payne's Grey/Alizarin Crimson mix the mountain structure projecting through the snow.

WET-IN-WET AND TISSUE

This group of rocks, typical of those to be found on a beach, were painted by applying several colours and tones and while the paint was still wet, with a tissue shaped to a wedge or point, paint was removed to reveal light areas. This is a very simple technique. A few fissures in the rock face were added with the rigger brush when the underpainting was dry.

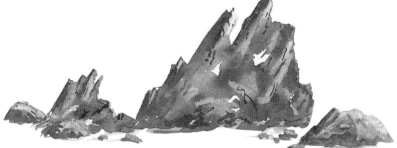

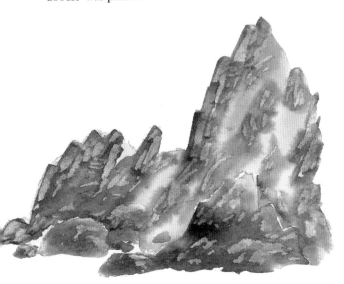

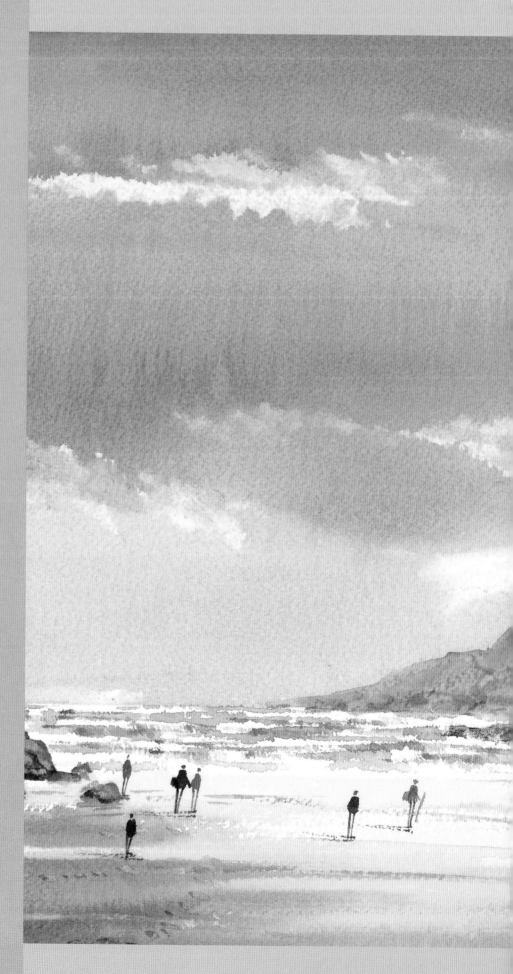

Right: A Walk on the Beach

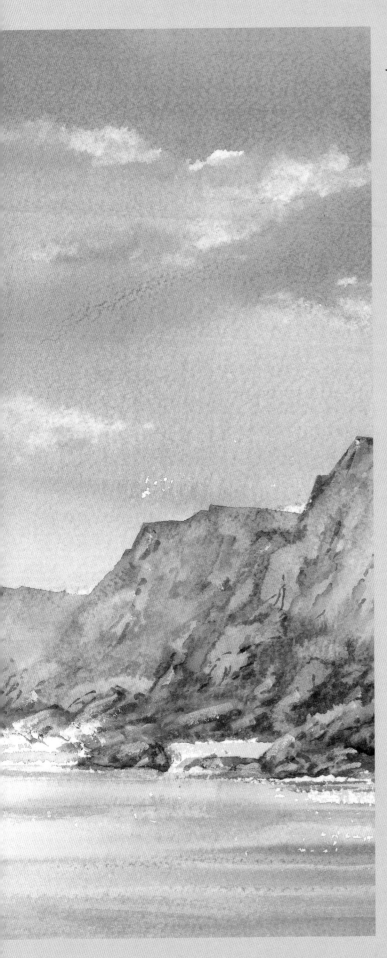

SUMMER

The thick roof

Of green and stirring branches is alive

And musical with birds that sing and sport

In wantonness of spirit; while below

The squirrel, with raised paws and form erect,

Chirps merrily. Throngs of insects in the shade

Try their thin wings and dance in the warm beam

That wake them into life. Even the green trees

Partake the deep contentment; as they bend

To the soft winds, the sun from the blue sky

Looks in and sheds a blessing on the scene.

William Cullen Bryant

Summer offers a wealth of subjects to both beginners and experienced artists. Look around and you will find much to inspire you.

The countryside is in full bloom; dog roses, meadowsweet, meadow cranesbill and poppies bring colour to the hedgerows and meadows. Cows and sheep graze in the pastures and as corn, wheat and barley ripen, acres of land turn gold in the sun.

If you have a garden you may not need to go out to find subjects from the natural world, since you are bound to find subjects there. Even if your garden isn't a riot of colour all through the summer months, you can still paint foliage, texture and colour, making landscapes in miniature.

YOSEMITE FALLS – CLOSE UP

This exercise cries out for the use of a palette knife to create the mountain structure; see pages 74–75 for technique.

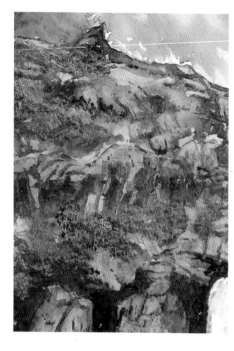

WHAT YOU WILL NEED

PAPER:
Winsor & Newton 640 gsm/300 lb Rough

BRUSHES:
Winsor & Newton Sceptre Gold II
Series 19 mm/¾ in flat, size 3 rigger,
38 mm/1½ in hake, size 6 round,
bristle brush

COLOURS:
Payne's Grey, Alizarin Crimson, Raw
Sienna, Burnt Sienna, Cadmium Yellow
Pale, Sap Green

SUPPORTIVE:
Palette knife, tissues, dark brown water-
soluble crayon

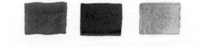

MOUNTAIN STRUCTURE

Having established the composition, a simple drawing was completed using the dark brown water-soluble crayon. It was then just a matter of splashing paint all over – that's a technical term!

Using a 19 mm/¾ in flat brush, an overall Raw Sienna wash was applied to the mountain areas, followed by washes of Burnt Sienna for warmth and dark values of a Payne's Grey/Alizarin Crimson mix to add depth. Think of the various mountain promontories as being parts of a jigsaw, painted separately, which as a whole establish the mountain.

When the paint is about one-third dry, use the palette knife to move paint to create the desired effect. This technique takes about five minutes.

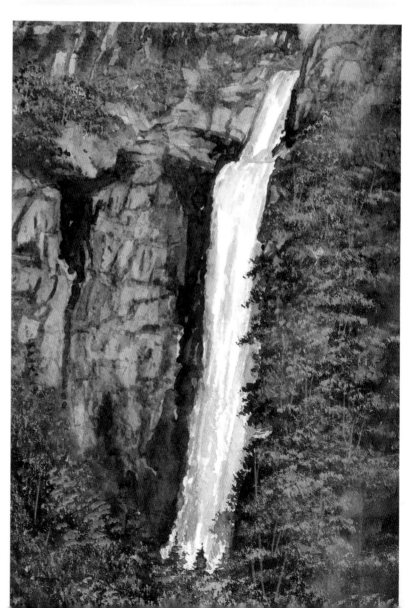

SKY AND TREES

The atmospheric sky was painted by applying a Payne's Grey/ Raw Sienna mix over a Raw Sienna underpainting. Finally, the trees were painted using the bristle brush.

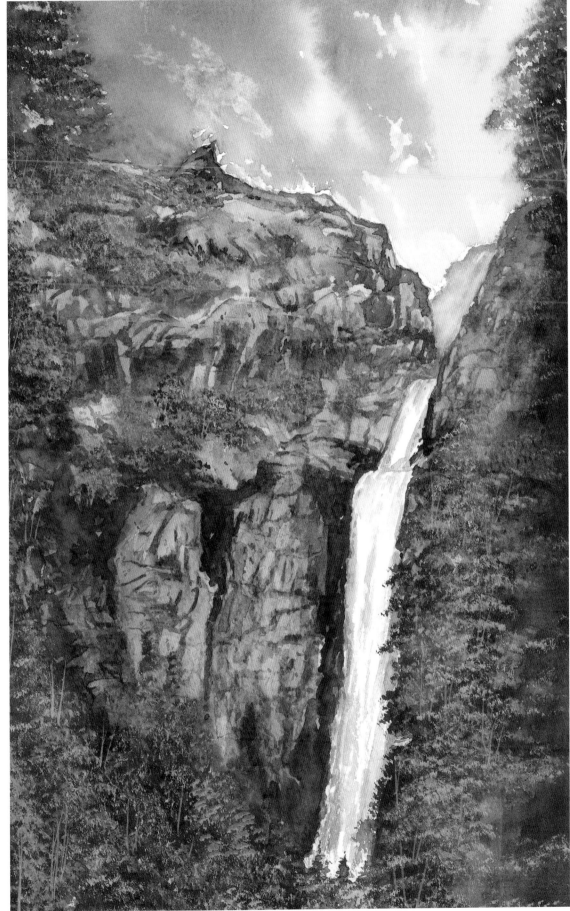

WATERFALL

The waterfall was painted with quick, light strokes from the hake brush, using the technique shown on page 67.

YOSEMITE FALLS – CLOSE UP

PRETTY HAMLET – PROJECT

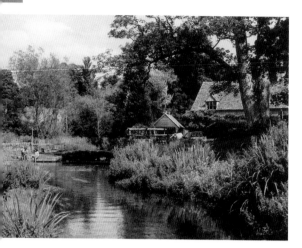

This pretty hamlet displays a wide range of greens, providing an opportunity to practise colour mixing. A scene such as this can be tricky for beginners, who can make the mistake of painting the trees as a mass and the riverbank as unvarying. The key is to observe the different tree species and any variations in the bank. If you paint each tree or bush as individuals, with their own structure, colour and form, when they are all linked together in the composition they will present a unified whole.

WHAT YOU WILL NEED

PAPER:
Winsor & Newton 640 gsm/300 lb Rough

BRUSHES:
Winsor & Newton Sceptre Gold II Series size 14 round, size 6 round, size 3 rigger, 19 mm/¾ in flat, 38 mm/1½ in hake

COLOURS:
Payne's Grey, French Ultramarine, Alizarin Crimson, Raw Sienna, Burnt Sienna, Burnt Umber, Cadmium Yellow Pale, Sap Green

SUPPORTIVE:
Masking fluid, natural sponge, 13 mm/½ in diameter oil painting brush

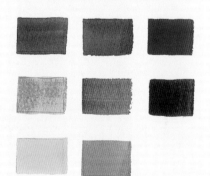

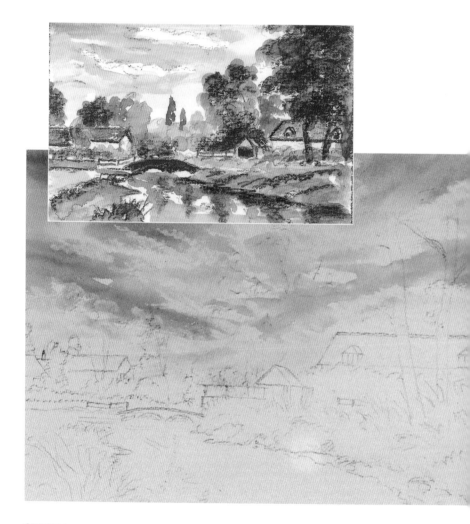

STAGE 1:

DRAWING, SKY AND MASKING

A dark brown water-soluble crayon was used for the outline, with care taken to accurately portray the relationship between the various elements and the correct angle and linear perspective of the river. Masking fluid was applied to the tree structures, window frames, tufts of grass and the light effects on the water. See Stage 9 for clarity.

I have painted a simple yet interesting cloud structure by applying the usual Raw Sienna wash and brushing in French Ultramarine with the hake brush. An absorbent tissue was used to remove paint to produce the soft white clouds.

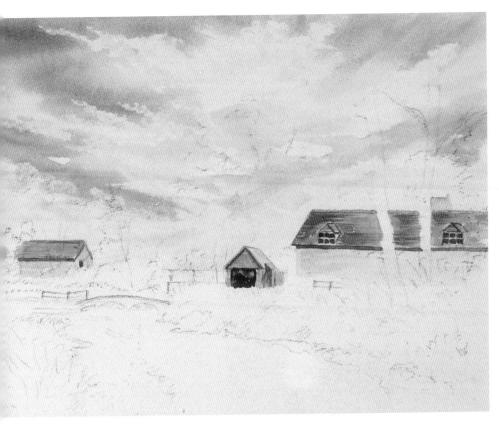

STAGE 2:
BUILDINGS

With the 19 mm/¾ in flat brush, paint the walls using Raw Sienna and the roofs of the buildings with a Burnt Sienna/Raw Sienna mix. Don't forget to paint shadows under the eaves. The windows and garage door were painted using a Payne's Grey/Alizarin Crimson mix. While this is still wet, dab the windows and door with a tissue shaped to a point to indicate light areas created by the sun.

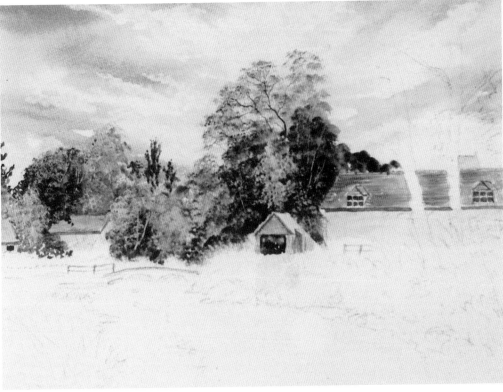

STAGE 3:
TREE AND BUSH FOLIAGE

An oil painter's brush is effective for stippling paint in various colours and values to create realistic foliage. Here, various tones of Raw Sienna, Sap Green and Cadmium Yellow Pale were used.

PRETTY HAMLET – PROJECT

82

STAGE 4:

TREE STRUCTURES

The masking was removed from the tree structures. The technique used to paint these structures initially is to apply a very pale Raw Sienna wash. When this wash is approximately one-third dry, using the edge of the 19 mm/¾ in flat brush loaded with Burnt Umber, move down the trunk depositing paint; lifting the brush every 1 cm/½ in and touching lightly will encourage the paint to blend with the damp underpainting. Use a tissue to remove paint where required to lighten areas and control the flow. The rigger brush was used to paint the branches.

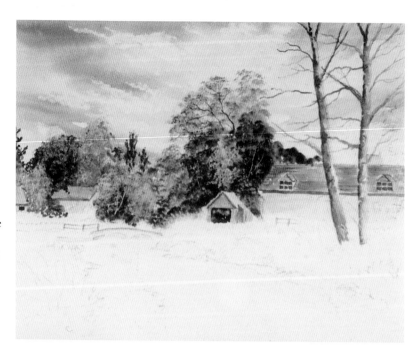

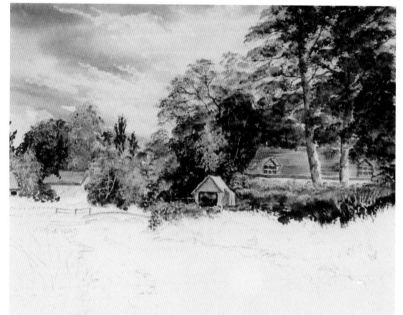

STAGE 5:

PAINTING MIDDLE DISTANCE AND TREE FOLIAGE

The hedge and darker values for the main tree foliage were painted with several tones of a Cadmium Yellow/Sap Green mix. A sponge was used to block in paint and the oil painter's hog hair brush was ideal to soften the edges and apply the light tones in the hedge.

STAGE 6:

RIGHT-HAND BANK

This needed to be built up gradually, leaving lighter values in appropriate areas. A pale Raw Sienna wash was applied overall, followed by various green values to indicate the distribution of the grass as it grows to the water's edge. The effect of the masking can easily be seen amid the grasses.

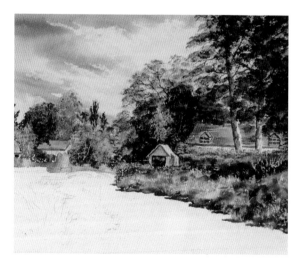

SUMMER

STAGE 7:

LEFT-HAND BANK AND BRIDGE

The left-hand bank was painted using the size 14 round brush. Washes of Raw Sienna, a soft green made from French Ultramarine/Cadmium Yellow and Burnt Sienna were applied to selected areas as shown in the photograph. The bridge outline was painted using a dark Burnt Umber value. The stone wall on the left was painted by applying washes of Raw Sienna, Burnt Sienna and Payne's Grey/Alizarin Crimson and the palette knife was used to create structure.

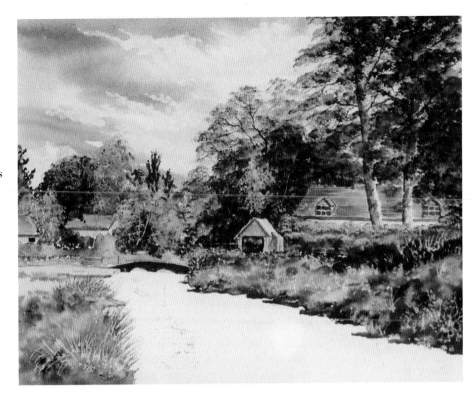

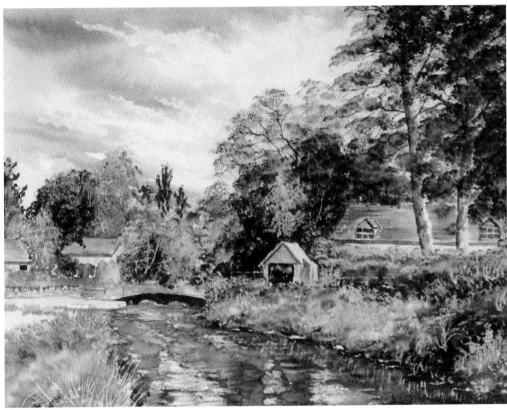

STAGE 8:

WATER AND TEXTURE

The water in this river is quite dark in value. I used the 38 mm/1½ in hake brush loaded with mixes of Raw Sienna/Burnt Sienna initially then overpainted with a Sap Green/Burnt Umber glaze.

More detail was stippled into the right-hand bank and tufts of reed growing through the water were added with Raw Sienna/Burnt Sienna mixes.

STAGE 9:
REMOVING THE MASKING

The masking was removed with a putty eraser, revealing the distant fence, the outline of the bridge, and the light effects on the water and tufts of grass.

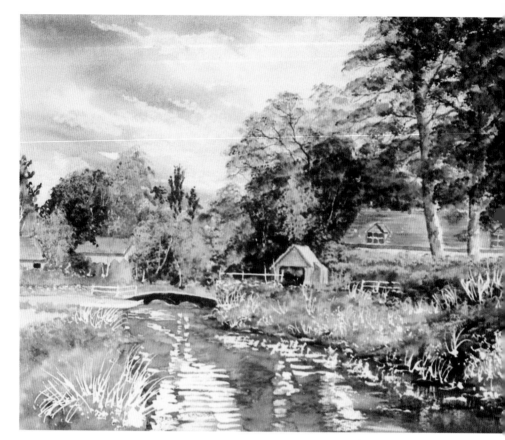

STAGE 10:
DETAILING THE BANKS

With a size 6 round brush loaded with a Payne's Grey/Alizarin Crimson mix, darker tones were painted into the banks, particularly the right-hand one, indicating the pattern and angle of growth of the grasses and other vegetation. .

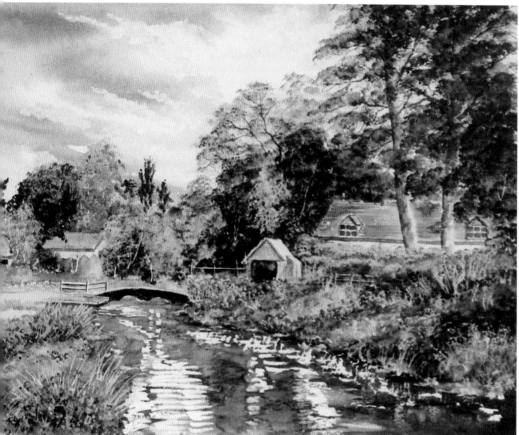

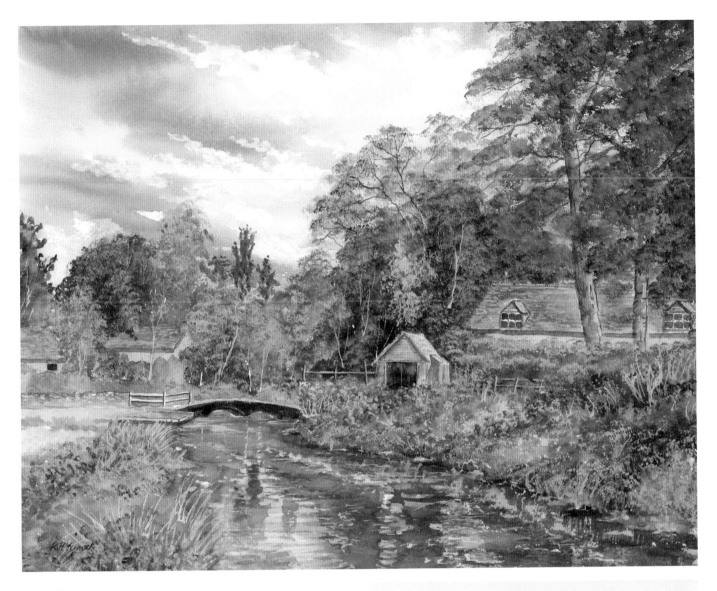

FINAL STAGE:

WATER AND HIGHLIGHTS

Touches of French Ultramarine were applied to the surface of the river and a little Burnt Sienna/Raw Sienna was brushed in, adding sparkle on the water.

White acrylic paint was added to the various mixes previously used, to add highlights in the tree foliage and vegetation on the riverbank.

KEY POINTS

1 Paint a simple but interesting sky.
2 Take care to paint the tree masses as being compiled of individual trees/bushes.
3 Add a variety of colours and tones to the foliage and in the vegetation on the riverbanks.
4 Build up the surface water gradually, by using washes and glazes.
5 Finally, add highlights to make the painting sparkle.
6 Notice that colour harmony and unity has been achieved by painting similar colours in most areas of the painting.

PERSPECTIVE – MADE SIMPLE

As artists, there are two types of perspective with which we need to concern ourselves – linear perspective and aerial perspective.

LINEAR PERSPECTIVE

The first, linear perspective, is particularly important when painting buildings. The easiest example of linear perspective is a railway line or road that appears to narrow as it stretches ahead until it vanishes on the horizon.

When you are painting buildings the same principle applies. Each feature – the roof, windows, ground level and so on – is angled to a vanishing point on the horizon, which is always at your eye level.

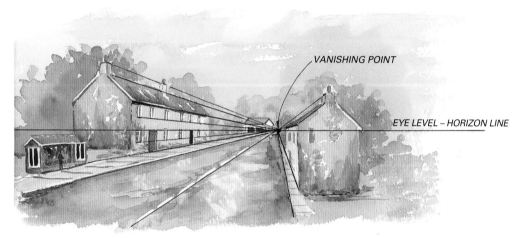

VANISHING POINT

EYE LEVEL – HORIZON LINE

ONE-POINT PERSPECTIVE

This occurs when one side of the building faces directly towards you, as in the sketch above.

The base of the wall facing you will appear horizontal but the roof, windows and side wall of the building will appear angled. The correct angle can be found by drawing lines from the top and bottom corners of the facing wall to the vanishing point.

TWO-POINT PERSPECTIVE

This occurs when the scene is viewed from the side rather than face on. There will be two vanishing points here, both on the horizon, though one or both may be off the paper. The same principles apply; the area between horizontal elements of the structure such as the rooflines and windows will appear to diminish as the building recedes from you.

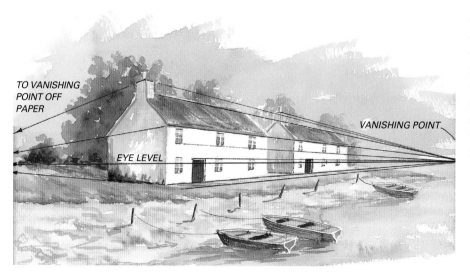

TO VANISHING POINT OFF PAPER

EYE LEVEL

VANISHING POINT

SIMPLIFYING

In practice all that is needed is to cut an aperture in a piece of mount card and view the scene. Position elastic bands around the perimeter of the card and align them with the various angles of the building features.

Then it's simply a matter of laying this over your paper and drawing along the elastic bands to transfer the true angles to your painting.

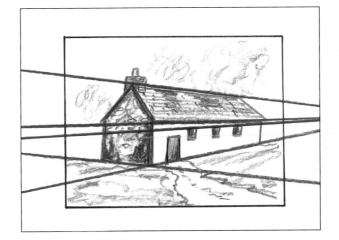

AERIAL PERSPECTIVE

This is of particular significance in order to achieve a sense of distance (recession) in a painting.

To give the appearance of recession in this sketch of a barn, the distant mountains are painted in cool colours, with little detail and light values. As the foreground is approached, warmer colours are used, more detail is painted and darker values are applied.

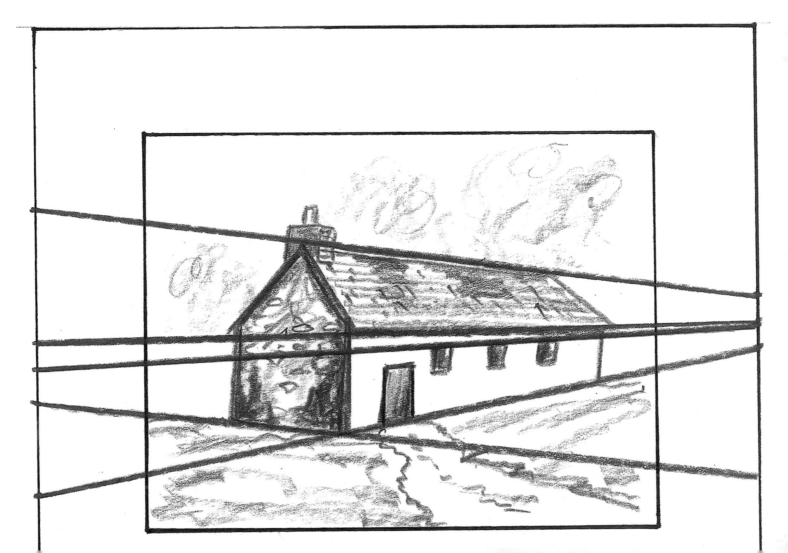

HIGHLANDS – PROJECT

This is a view of the valley of Glencoe, in the Scottish Highlands. I have included this scene to provide practice in painting mountain structures. It is important to identify the main promontories and peaks as well as the gullies and fissures, but don't attempt to copy the structure exactly – simplify, discarding small details that don't contribute significantly to the structure.

I find a small pair of binoculars useful for identifying areas of the mountain in shadow. If I paint what I see at the time, the mountain may look completely different in a changing light. I need to know whether the shadow area is a deep gully or simply a cloud shadow. I want the structure to be reasonably representational.

The photograph shows the view and the tonal study is the first stage in helping to determine the accuracy of the structure. It makes me question the specific features and determines the value patterns.

The large area of trees requires a sympathetic representation. This is always a difficult mass to paint; the best approach is to use a variety of values and colours and to indicate the structure of a few trees in the foreground.

The wild flowers were added for interest. I visit this area regularly, but at the time the photograph was taken the flowers were not in bloom.

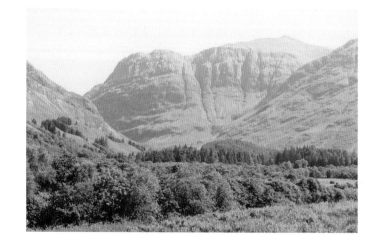

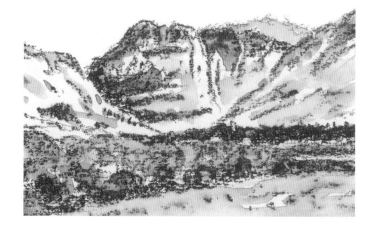

WHAT YOU WILL NEED

PAPER:
Saunders Waterford 640 gsm/300 lb Rough

BRUSHES:
Winsor & Newton Sceptre Gold II Series size 6 round, size 14 round, 19 mm/¾ in flat, 38 mm/1½ in hake, 13 mm/½ in diameter hog hair

COLOURS:
Payne's Grey, Cobalt Blue, Alizarin Crimson, Raw Sienna, Cadmium Yellow Pale, Sap Green

SUPPORTIVE:
Dark brown water-soluble crayon, old toothbrush, 25 mm/1 in masking tape, palette knife

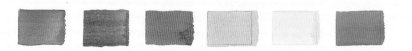

STAGE 1:
DRAWING AND SKY

A water-soluble crayon was used to draw the main features. The sky was painted by brushing Cobalt Blue/Alizarin Crimson into a Raw Sienna underpainting wet-in-wet, using the 38 mm/1½ in hake brush.

STAGE 2:
DISTANT MOUNTAINS

This is the tricky part. Paint an area at a time – it can't be rushed. Begin with a Raw Sienna wash and using a size 14 round brush, paint in a Payne's Grey/Cobalt Blue mix to create the mountain structure, commencing with the main promontories and gullies. Establish their positions and paint the fissures around them. This task needs to be done with care – stand back and view your efforts before progressing to the next area.

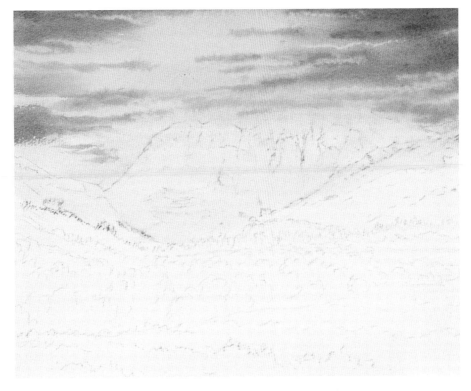

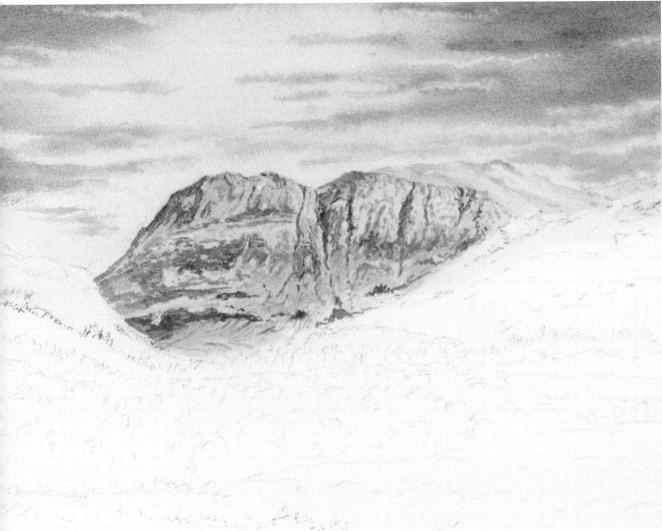

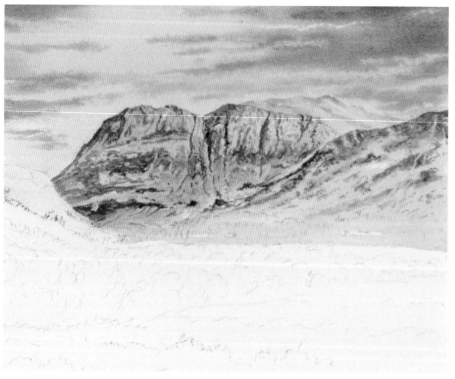

STAGE 3:
FOREGROUND MOUNTAIN

Apply a weak wash of Raw Sienna/Sap Green and while it is still wet, paint in the promontories with a Cobalt Blue/Sap Green mix. Use a size 6 round brush to push the paint around, softening the edges.

STAGE 4:
MOUNTAIN, DISTANT TREES

Paint the left-hand mountain, adding a little Burnt Umber to the mix when painting the promontories making up the structure of the mountain. When dry, paint the distant fir trees using the corner and edge of a 19 mm/¾ in flat brush loaded with a Payne's Grey/Sap Green mix with a little Cobalt Blue added. These techniques are shown on page 99.

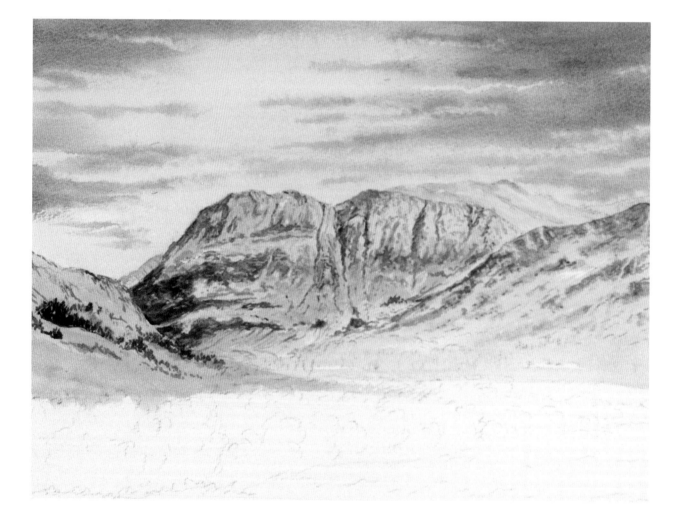

SUMMER

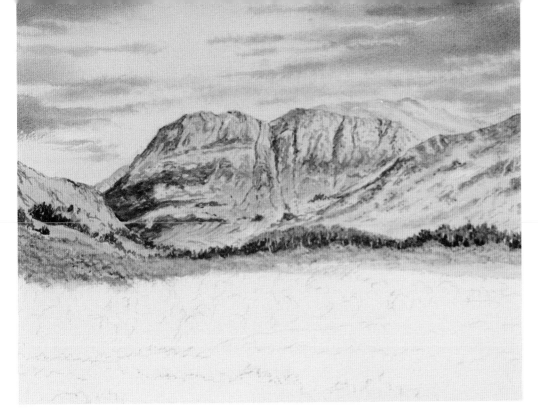

STAGE 5:
MIDDLE-DISTANCE TREES

Paint these with the edge of the 19 mm/¾ in flat brush, using a stippling action, and scratch out a few tree structures with your thumbnail, cocktail stick or palette knife. A useful tip is to stretch a piece of 25 mm/1 in masking tape across the paper to represent the base of the tree mass. Bend the tape when positioning to create an uneven effect. The colours used were a mix of Sap Green and Raw Sienna.

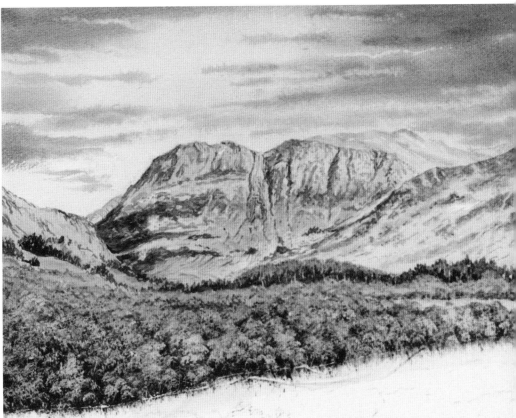

STAGE 6:
TREE MASS

The masking tape I stretched across the paper can be easily seen in the photograph. This enables me to paint over the tape, and on its removal, the top of the field has a clean line.

The trees were painted by stippling with a hog hair brush, using combinations of Raw Sienna, Cadmium Yellow Pale and Sap Green. The dark shadows, important for depth, were a mix of Payne's Grey and Alizarin Crimson. Scratch in a few tree trunks with a palette knife.

KEY POINTS

1 Produce a value pattern – it becomes the plan for your painting. Getting the lights and darks right is important, particularly when it comes to making the structure of the mountain look real.

2 Paint a simple sky because there is so much detail elsewhere in this landscape.

3 Take time to draw the profile of the mountain correctly.

4 Carefully note the shape of the peaks, promontories, gullies and fissures in the mountain.

5 Don't rush the painting of the mountain structure; take time to stand back and look before progressing further.

6 Detail a few tree structures at the front of the woodland.

7 Create an impression of rough texture in the foreground.

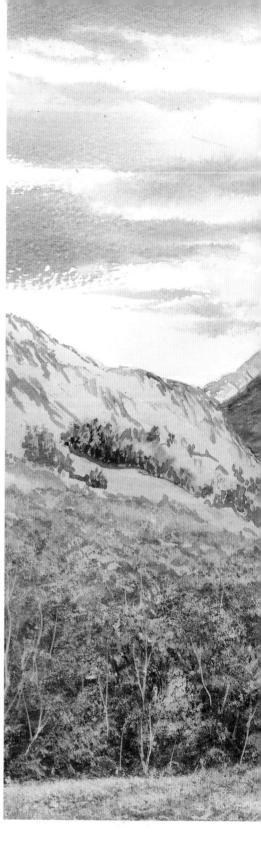

STAGE 7:

FOREGROUND

I wanted this area to look natural and untended. Initially a Raw Sienna/Cadmium Yellow wash was applied with the hake brush and when dry, darker values were stippled using the hog hair brush. Payne's Grey and Sap Green were added to the wash to create a variety of values. The hog hair brush gives the effect of rough grass. When the paint was dry, I painted a few lighter values by adding a little white acrylic to Cadmium Yellow Pale.

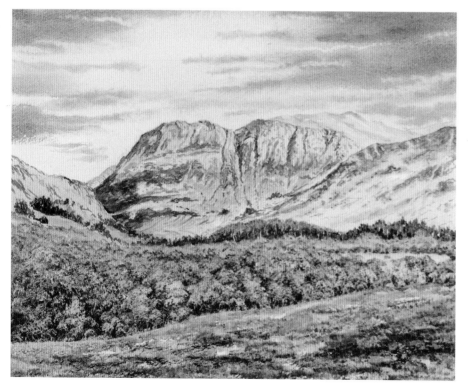

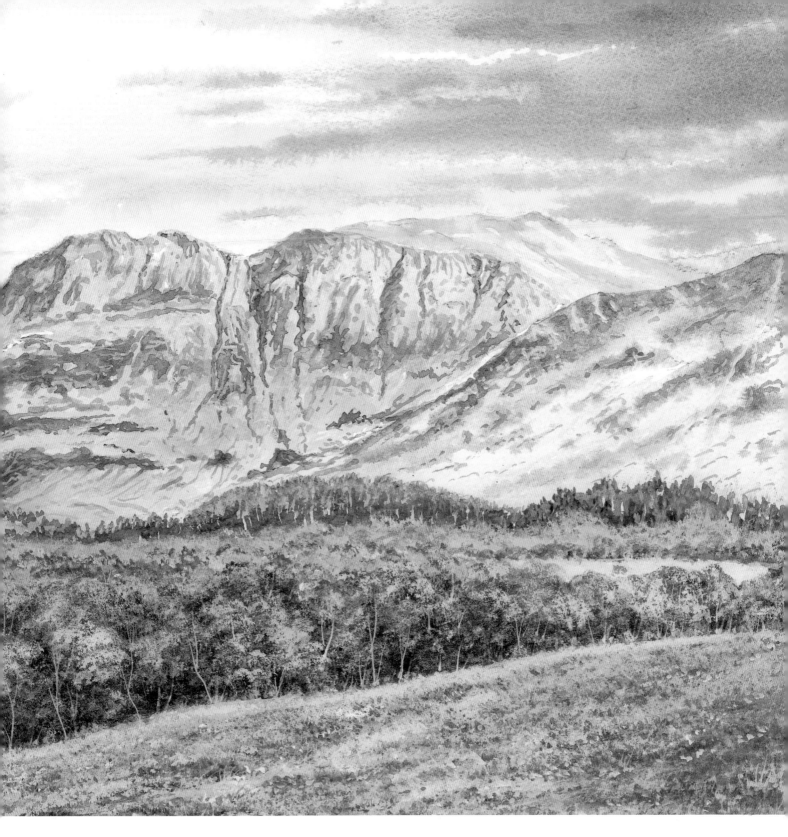

FINAL STAGE:
WILD FLOWERS

With the hog hair brush, I completed the painting by adding a few wild flowers. Reds, yellows and white were used here. The trees were masked with a sheet of newspaper and, using an old toothbrush dipped in paint, a few impressions of flowers were spattered into the foreground by rubbing my thumb across the bristles.

FARMSTEAD – CLOSE UP

This upland farmstead is typical of the rural buildings in the English Lake District. The farm has a round chimney, which in this region signifies its age. As is the case with most farms, the house has a cluster of agricultural barns and other outbuildings around it, some in the local stone and others more modern in appearance.

WHAT YOU WILL NEED

PAPER:
Saunders Waterford 640 gsm/300 lb rough

BRUSHES:
Winsor & Newton Sceptre Gold II Series size 14 round, size 3 rigger, 19 mm/¾ in flat, 38 mm/1½ in hake, size 6 round hog hair brush

COLOURS:
Payne's Grey, Cerulean Blue, Alizarin Crimson, Burnt Umber, Cadmium Yellow Pale, Sap Green, Raw Sienna

SUPPORTIVE:
Palette knife, white acrylic paint, tissues

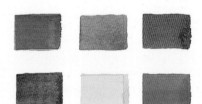

SKY
The wet-in-wet sky was painted by brushing in Cerulean Blue/Alizarin Crimson over a Raw Sienna underpainting.

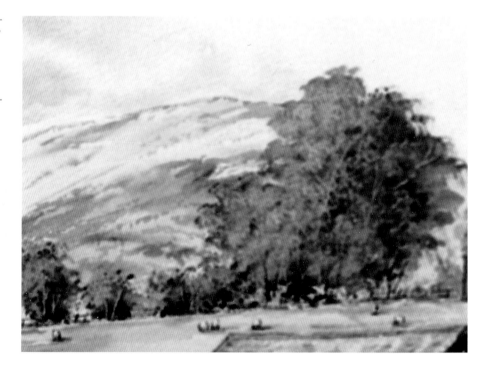

MOUNTAINS AND TREES
The mountain was painted wet-in-wet by dropping various values of green into a Raw Sienna underpainting. I painted the tree grouping by applying downward strokes with the side of the size 14 round brush for the underpainting and when the paint was about one-third dry, a lighter value was stippled with a hog hair brush to represent highlights on the foliage. The tree structure was scratched in using a palette knife.

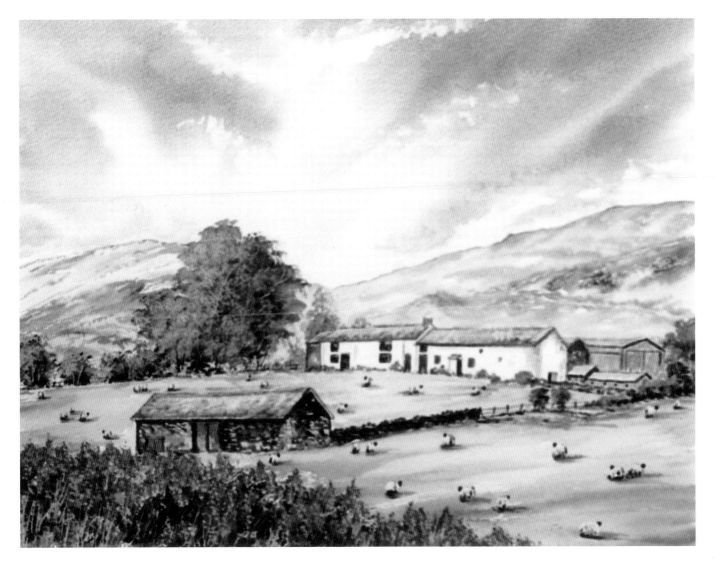

BARN AND FLOWERS

The stonework of the barn and wall was created by applying several washes, beginning with a Raw Sienna underpainting and adding Burnt Umber, followed by a Payne's Grey/Alizarin Crimson mix. While these were still wet, a palette knife was used to move paint, giving the impression of stonework. The rose bay willowherbs in the foreground are to be found growing throughout the region and add colour to this landscape.

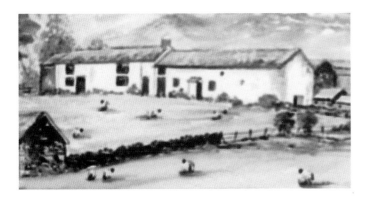

BUILDING

I used the 19 mm/¾ in flat brush to paint the farmhouse. In the Lake District, farmhouses are traditionally white faced structures with green/grey roofs and are usually connected to stone built outbuildings or barns.

To paint the Lakeland sheep, which are often Herdwicks, Swaledales or Scottish Blackface breed, simply paint horseshoes (see page 117). Those shown are Scottish Blackface.

HOW TO PAINT TREES

Almost every landscape painting will include one or more trees. It is important, therefore, that they are painted reasonably accurately in terms of shape, size and value. Observe the direction of the light and add highlights to your finished work.

Trees appear dark on the inside and light on the outside. The watercolourist is told to paint from light to dark, which is the opposite of trees in nature.

I refuse to be bound by old rules and paint my trees in the conventional way or by applying a dark underpainting, and when dry, building up the groups of light foliage. Finally, I paint the highlights by adding a little white acrylic paint or gouache to colour, ensuring the final highlights don't sink into the watercolour paper. The choice is yours.

When painting trees, study their structures; an ideal time to do this is in winter when the leaves have fallen. Their trunks have to be sufficiently sturdy to support the boughs. These hold the branches that in turn radiate thinner twigs that reach outwards to catch the light.

Tree trunks vary significantly in colour according to tree type, weather conditions and season. A wet tree trunk will look completely different to one that is dry with sunlight shining on it. The colours may vary from greys through browns to Burnt Sienna. When painting tree trunks, I find an effective technique is to wet the area initially with a pale wash and when it is about one-third dry, add darker values and allow the colours to blend together. While they are still wet, use an absorbent tissue to remove paint to represent highlights. This technique is very effective!

While artists do not need to know the names of the trees they are painting, their structure and form must be represented accurately. It is obvious that a poplar tree is different to a palm tree, which is different to an oak tree and so on. Try painting trees with different brushes and techniques. Over the following pages I shall show you several techniques I use to represent them, but in this book it is not my intention to attempt to impose a style of painting upon you; I couldn't even if I tried. You and only you will decide whether you wish to paint loosely or in detail. However, if you practise these techniques, you will soon be able to paint trees that look realistic and you can go on to develop your own style.

PAINTING A SPECIMEN TREE

Stage 1
Begin by painting a base colour to help establish the shape.

Stage 2
Apply darker tones to create depth. Paint in a few branches and the trunk, which should look sufficiently sturdy to carry the boughs.

Stage 3
Paint impressions of foliage and add highlights.

COLOURS USED

For summer trees use mixes of Cadmium Yellow Pale, Raw Sienna, Cobalt Blue, Sap Green and Payne's Grey. For autumn trees use mixes of Cadmium Yellow Pale, Raw Sienna, Cadmium Orange, Burnt Sienna, Alizarin Crimson and Payne's Grey.

BRUSHES

Try a 19 mm/¾ in flat or the side of a size 14 round. Finish by stippling with a sponge or old oil painter's hog hair brush.

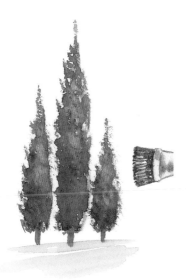

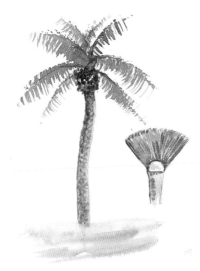

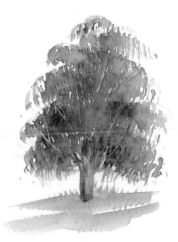

POPLAR trees tend to be tall, with a dense leaf canopy. Vary their height in a painting.

Paint them using the edge of a 19 mm/¾ in flat brush. Hold it almost at right angles to the paper and work with a stippling technique.

PALM trees are tall and graceful, with rough-textured trunks and open fronds growing from the top.

Paint the fronds by producing a thin curved line with a fan brush and then flicking downwards to create the open foliage.

WILLOWS are a varied genus, but most are painted as being of the weeping shape with graceful, pendent, lace-like foliage. Paint them with a fan brush or hake brush made of very soft hair.

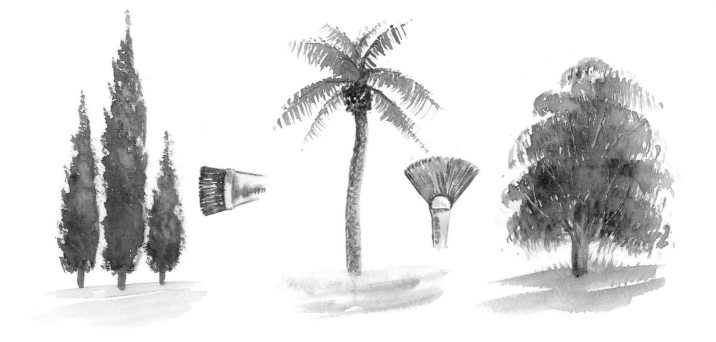

To paint the effects of snow on trees, initially apply a deposit of masking fluid. In this example, I have shaped a piece of tissue to a point, dipped it into masking fluid and stippled.

When the masking is dry, it can be overpainted. When the overpainting is completely dry, remove the masking with a putty eraser and the trees appear to be laden with snow. It is as simple as that. Note that I have masked a few thin lines representing tree structures: alternatively, these could have been painted in at the end, using a cocktail stick dipped in white acrylic paint.

HOW TO PAINT TREES

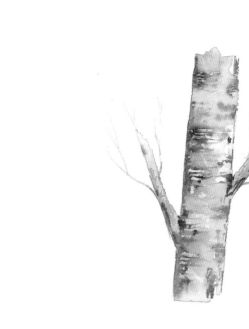

The tree structure above was painted by applying a Raw Sienna wash and brushing in some Burnt Sienna and Burnt Umber while that was still wet. A size 6 round brush can be used either to move paint around or, when clean and dry, to soak up paint by absorption.

To create texture on the beech trunk (top right) a grey wash was applied. When it was one-third dry Burnt Sienna and Burnt Umber were brushed in. Once dry, a rigger brush was used to add detail.

To achieve recession, paint distant trees in cool colours and foreground trees in warmer colours in more detail. The tree mass below was painted wet-in-wet. The background trees were painted using downward twitches with the side of the size 14 round brush, varying the values with cool colours for the distant trees and gradually warmer values for the middle-distance trees. A palette knife was used to scratch in some tree structures when the paint was approximately one-third dry.

The specimen tree was painted by dipping a 19 mm/¾ in flat brush into three colours at once and using twisting, downward strokes of the brush. At the top of the tree, Raw Sienna was loaded on one side of the brush, Burnt Sienna on the other side and Burnt Umber along the edge. Press the brush on to the paper and turn it, changing sides as required to create variation/gradation in the foliage. At lower levels, Raw Sienna, Cadmium Yellow and Sap Green was used in the same manner.

✍ Hold the brush flat and horizontal to the paper and simply twitch it in a downward direction, lightly depositing paint. Apply at least three values from light to dark.

✍ Hold a 19 mm/¾ in flat brush loaded with paint at right angles to the paper. Stipple from side to side, working upward from the base. To achieve the shape, use more of the corners of the brush as you work nearer the top of the tree.

✍ An old, worn oil painter's brush is ideal for stippling foliage.

✍ Try a piece of crumpled greaseproof paper or tissue to stipple paint.

✍ A natural sponge is a useful aid to create the effects of foliage and texture. Apply at least three values. Do not squeeze the sponge as you stipple.

HOW TO PAINT TREES

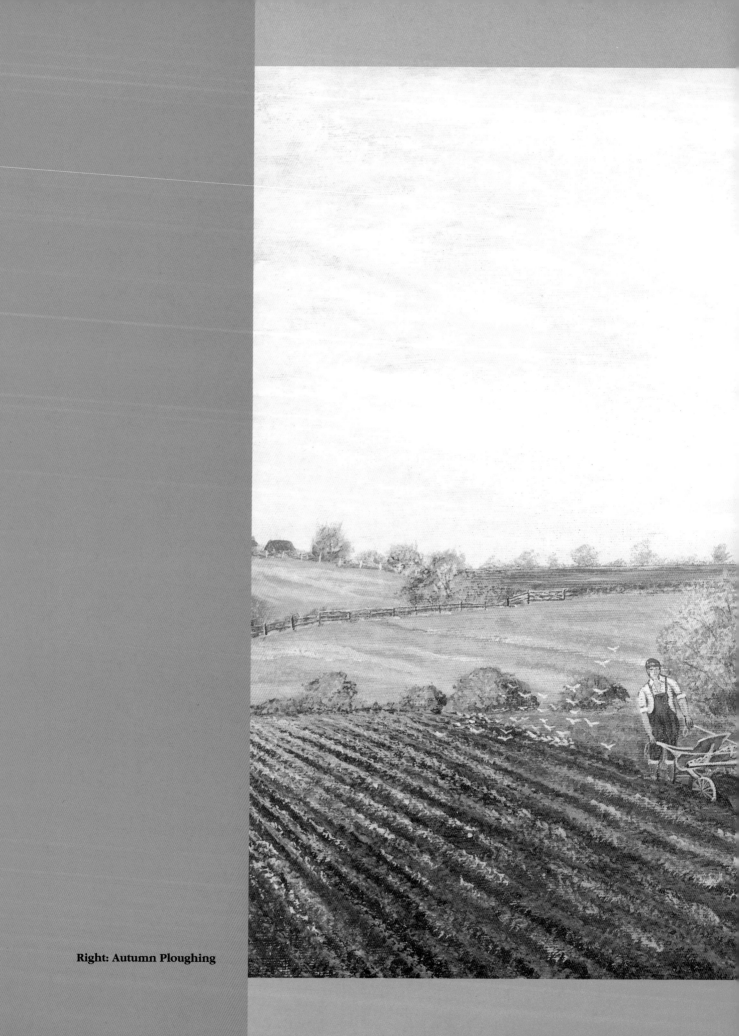

Right: Autumn Ploughing

Season of mists and mellow fruitfulness
Close bosom-friend of the maturing sun;
Conspiring with him how to load and bless
With fruit the vines that round the thatch-eves run;
To bend with apples the moss'd cottage-trees
And fill all fruit with ripeness to the core;
To swell the gourd and plump the hazel shells
With a sweet kernel; to set budding more,
And still more, later flowers for the bees,
Until they think warm days will never cease,
For Summer has o'er brimm'd their damming cells.

John Keats

Autumn is a wonderful time of year to paint. The summer greens evolve into a panorama of yellows, sienna and russet reds before the leaf fall creates a carpet of sparkling colour. It's the season of brightly coloured berries too, in orange, purple and red on trees and in hedgerows.

With autumn rains, the rivers are often in full spate and waterfalls are increasingly dramatic. Dampness and mist often cover the landscape and the days become shorter, allowing the artist less time for al fresco painting. Nevertheless, there are ample subjects to inspire both the beginner and the experienced artist.

AUTUMN PASTURE – PROJECT

This is one of those exercises that provides an opportunity to demonstrate the three ingredients of a successful painting; in this case, an atmospheric sky, an interesting group of bushes in the middle distance and a colourful foreground with plenty of texture.

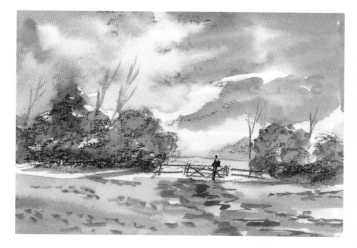

The tonal study was completed in order to establish the value relationships.

WHAT YOU WILL NEED

PAPER:
Winsor & Newton 640 gsm/300 lb Rough

BRUSHES:
Winsor & Newton Sceptre Gold II Series size 14 round, size 3 rigger, 38 mm/1½ in hake, size 6 round, hog hair

PAINTS:
Payne's Grey, French Ultramarine, Alizarin Crimson, Raw Sienna, Burnt Sienna, Cadmium Yellow Pale, Sap Green

SUPPORTIVE:
Masking tape, white acrylic paint, tissues

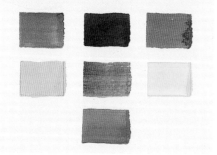

STAGE 1:

SKY

The initial stage is to fix the horizon line by positioning a piece of 25 mm/1 in masking tape across the paper. Note that the tape has been bent to create a horizon line that is not perfectly level, as would be the case in reality.

The sky was painted using the 38 mm/1½ in hake brush and a Raw Sienna wash. When the shine had left the underpainting, the clouds were painted using a French Ultramarine /Payne's Grey mix.

Create interesting cloud shapes by using a tissue to remove paint with a dabbing action to improve their structures.

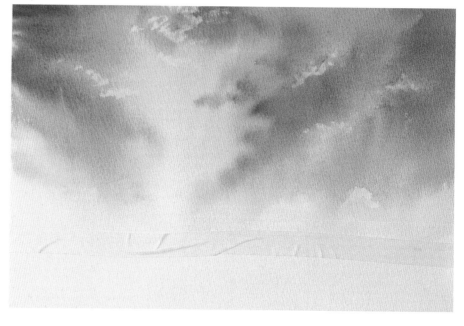

STAGE 2:

BUSHES

Use an old, round hog hair brush to stipple in the form of the bushes. Make them different heights and use a variety of colours mixed from Cadmium Yellow Pale, French Ultramarine, Raw Sienna, Burnt Sienna, Alizarin Crimson and Payne's Grey. Practise your colour mixes first on a piece of watercolour paper. Work from light to dark, quite wet, allowing the colours to blend together. Paint in the fence and gate. In order to lead the viewer's eye into the distance, paint a few distant bushes beyond the gate.

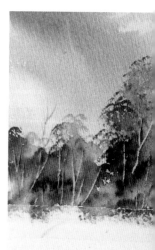

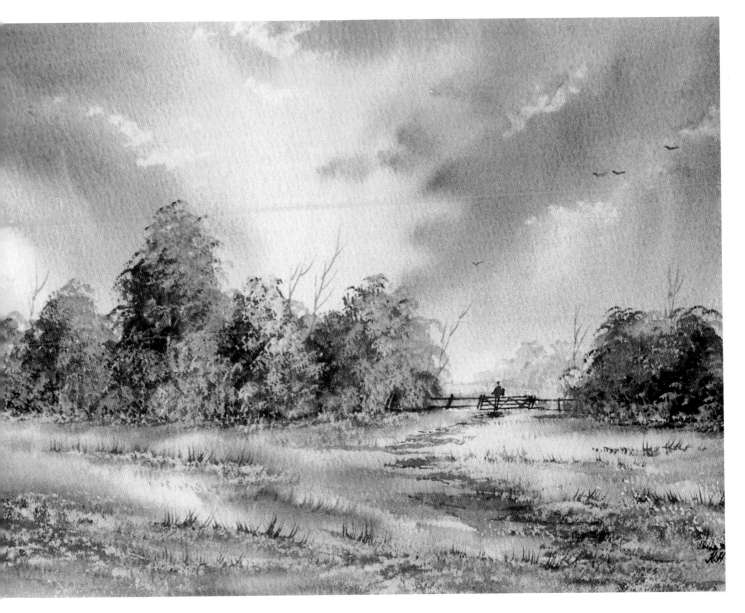

STAGE 3:
BUSHES AND FOREGROUND

Carefully remove the masking tape. Add more detail to the bushes, in particular highlights created by adding a little white acrylic paint to the mixes, ensuring that the highlights remain on the top of the paper, rather than sink in and lose the necessary sparkle.

The foreground needs to be sensitively painted by initially applying a weak Raw Sienna wash over the whole of the foreground. Brush a little Burnt Sienna in and a Payne's Grey/Alizarin Crimson mix to represent shadows. When the underpainting is dry, use the edge of the hake brush to touch the paper, lightly depositing paint and flicking upwards to create the impression of stubble. Add darker tones to shape the path.

When the paint is dry, use an old worn hog hair brush to stipple in soft green colour, representing low-growing plants. Finally, add the figure and a few birds.

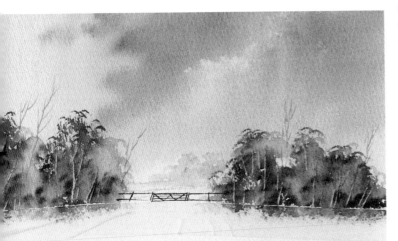

ON THE MOUNTAINS – PROJECT

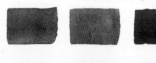
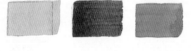

I have included this project as a demonstration of how to capture in paint the subtle colours of a mountain landscape. This particular subject also gives me an opportunity to describe how a realistic foreground is created.

Here the softness and variation in a mountain structure is captured and also the roughness and detail of a mountain foreground.

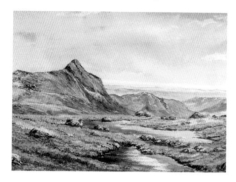

STAGE 1:

DRAWING, MASKING, SKY

Care was taken while drawing the outline, using a water-soluble crayon. It's important to capture a mountain profile as closely as possible, as walkers who may see your painting can be very critical. Artistic licence allows the repositioning of a few rocks, but if you are representing a particular mountain it must be accurate.

Masking fluid was applied to create highlights on the mountains and light on the rocks.

The sky was painted using the hake brush, as it is ideal to cover large areas of paper quickly, to avoid hard edges occurring. An initial wash of Raw Sienna was applied, followed by varying tones of Cobalt Blue – darker tones being applied to the top right to balance the main mountain structure on the left. A tissue was used to wipe out a few white clouds. A sky needs to be painted in less than three minutes to avoid hard edges occurring.

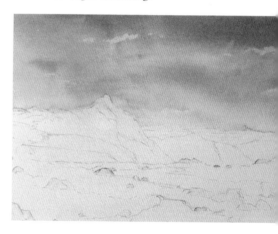

STAGE 2:

FOUNDATION FOR MOUNTAIN

Here I have used two brushes – the hake for sweeping washes and the 19 mm/¾ in flat brush for shaping the peaks. Using the hake brush, a Raw Sienna wash was applied to the whole of the mountain and a Raw Sienna/Sap Green mix applied to selected areas while they were still wet. Finally, prior to the paint becoming more than one-third dry, the flat brush was loaded with a Payne's Grey/Alizarin Crimson mix and used to shape the peaks and add darker values to the mountain.

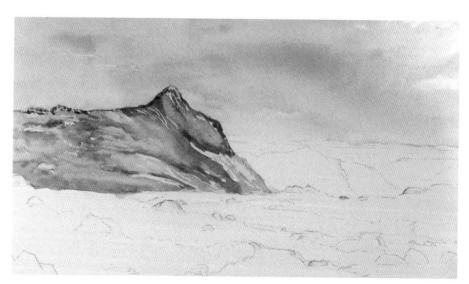

AUTUMN

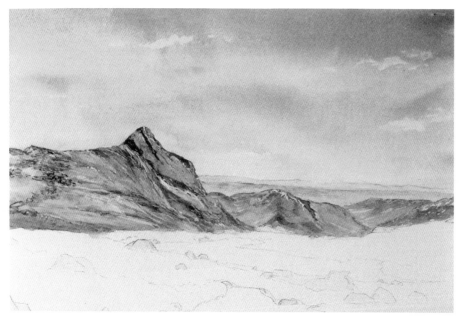

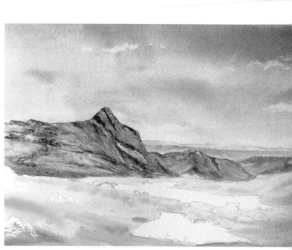

STAGE 3:
COMPLETING THE MOUNTAINS

The distant mountain ranges were painted using pale values of Cobalt Blue in the far distance with a hint of the Payne's Grey/Alizarin Crimson mix here and there. The middle-distance mountains were painted by applying a Raw Sienna underpainting, followed by various tonal values of Payne's Grey/Alizarin Crimson. The masking was removed using a putty eraser and detail added using a size 6 round brush.

On the left of the peak there is a group of rocks that lead to the top edge. A Payne's Grey/Alizarin Crimson was applied and allowed to soften the underpainting. A palette knife was used to move paint to represent the variety of shapes and sizes of rocks leading to the edge. The result of the foregoing process is a subtle blending of colour and a realistic representation of the mountain peak.

STAGE 4:
FOREGROUND WASHES

Using the hake brush, a weak Raw Sienna wash was applied to the whole of the foreground, followed by the application of Burnt Sienna to selected areas.

STAGE 5:
APPLYING DARKER VALUES

The edge of the hake brush is useful for painting rough grasses and texture. The loaded brush is simply tapped across the paper to deposit paint, rather like a stippling action. The edge of the brush is held at an angle approximately 30 degrees to the paper and by patting down on the paper the required effects are created. Just dance across the paper in this manner, remembering to use a light touch, having loaded the brush with less wet colours – greens, browns and sienna, all made from Sap Green, Raw Sienna and Burnt Sienna.

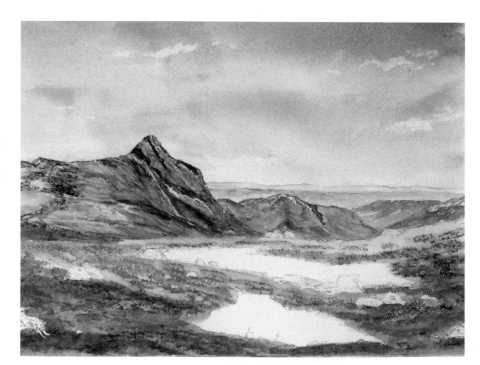

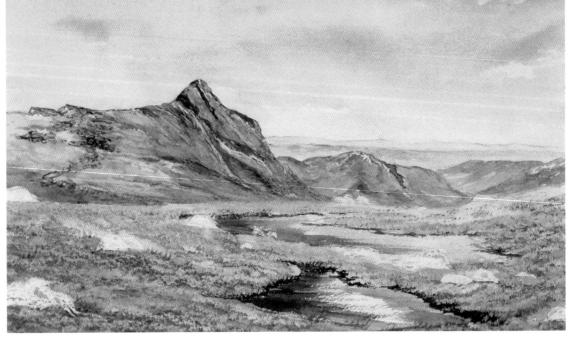

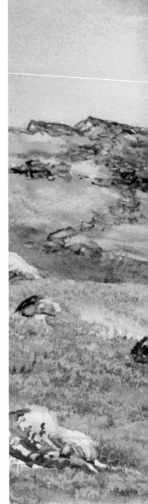

STAGE 6:
FOREGROUND

Using an oil painter's hog hair brush, the impression of rough texture was created by stippling with a little white acrylic/Raw Sienna mix, creating lighter areas of rough texture. The water was painted by using the side of the size 14 round brush, loaded with Cobalt Blue. A little Payne's Grey was added for the darker tones. The sparkle on the water was created by leaving the tooth of the paper uncovered – dry brush effect.

STAGE 7:
ROCKS

The rocks were painted using dark values of a Payne's Grey/Burnt Sienna mix and when dry the masking was removed. The size 6 round brush was used to add detail to the rocks.

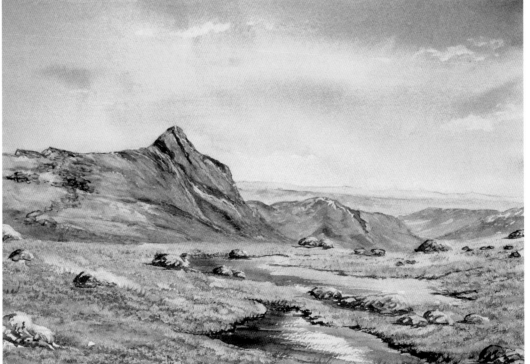

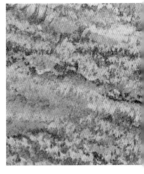

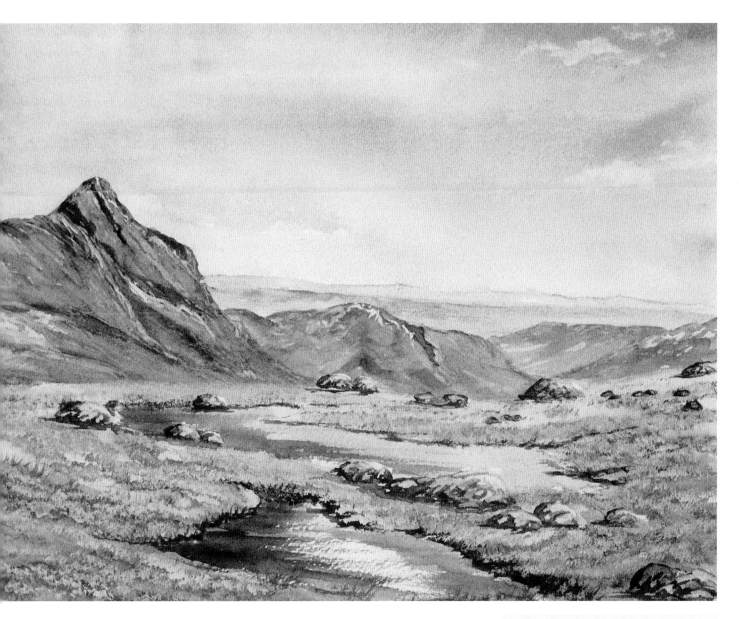

FINAL STAGE:
FINAL DETAILS

Darker values were added to represent shadows over the foreground and to edge the banks of the small areas of water. Note the tufts of grass growing over the rocks, painted by fanning the size 14 round brush and flicking in an upward direction. The rocks weren't placed there yesterday: there will be vegetation growing around their base. It's these small yet important details which separate the professional from the amateur painter.

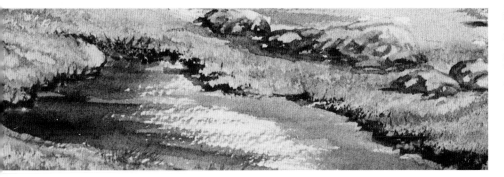

KEY POINTS

1 Paint a simple sky. Remember the golden rule – a detailed foreground requires a simple sky.
2 When painting the mountain structures, apply the washes and glazes wet-in-wet to allow the colours to blend together, creating soft texture.
3 Use an old hog hair brush to create texture in the foreground.
4 Add small details like the tufts of grass growing around the rocks for realism.

ON THE MOUNTAINS – PROJECT

COUNTRY LANE – CLOSE UP

This landscape has been included to provide experience in the painting of foreground texture. There are many techniques that I could have used to achieve the effect of rough grasses, wild plants, fallen leaves and the variation and gradation to be found on such roadside banks. I could have used a sponge, spattered paint, stippled or dabbed with a small brush or even combined all these techniques. I was attracted to this landscape because the track vanishes into the distance, beyond a stone building with red doors and roof, providing the focal point in this painting. This is one of those exceptions where although the focal point is only just off-centre, I feel it still works. The viewing points were very limited, due to the narrowness of the lane and the steep banks, and it was important to select a viewpoint where I could observe the track passing the building and going out of the painting.

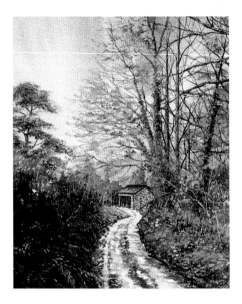

WHAT YOU WILL NEED

PAPER:
Winsor & Newton 640 gsm/300 lb Rough

BRUSHES:
Winsor & Newton Sceptre Gold II Series size 14 round, size 6 round, size 3 rigger, 38 mm/1½ in hake, hog hair

COLOURS:
Payne's Grey, Cobalt Blue, Alizarin Crimson, Raw Sienna, Burnt Sienna, Cadmium Yellow Pale, Sap Green

SUPPORTIVE:
Masking fluid, cocktail stick, natural sponge

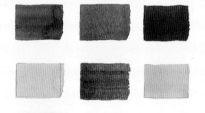

SKY

Because of the amount of detail in this landscape the sky needs to be painted simply. Using the hake brush a Raw Sienna wash was applied and Cobalt Blue brushed in – the brush strokes being directed towards the focal point, which is the building.

PINE TREE

This was a lovely shape, which helped to balance the right-hand tree group. I applied a soft green initially to represent the foliage and overpainted it while it was still wet, using a Payne's Grey/Sap Green mix to create depth. After the foliage had been painted, the tree trunk and branches were added, using the rigger brush and Burnt Umber.

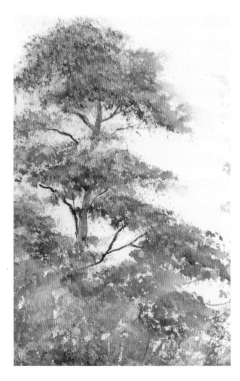

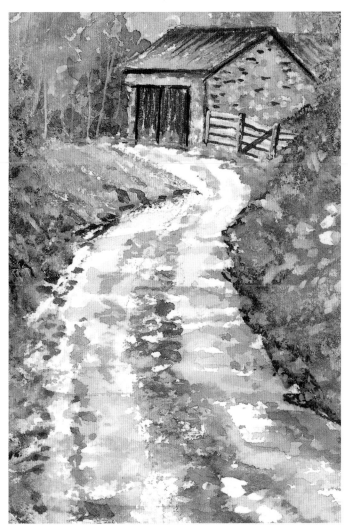

TRACK AND BUILDING

The track curved nicely up to the building and continued out of the painting. This was a rutted track and I wanted to indicate this roughness in the painting. I have left much of the paper uncovered as the track needed to appear light in tone to provide counterchange with the banks, which were painted a darker value. Using the size 14 round brush, Raw Sienna was washed in. When it was dry I used the side of the rigger brush loaded with a Payne's Grey/Alizarin Crimson mix to paint the texture on the track. The building was made of stone, depicted by applying a Raw Sienna underpainting and adding Payne's Grey and Burnt Sienna to emphasize a few of the stone shapes. An Alizarin Crimson/Burnt Sienna mix was used to paint the roof and doors.

TREES

The tree structures were painted with the rigger brush. When dry, a sponge was used to stipple various values of a Burnt Sienna/Raw Sienna mix. When that was dry the ivy growing up the trunks was painted by adding a light green followed by a darker value to indicate the depth of shadow.

Take care to ensure that the twigs on the trees are finely painted - there's nothing worse than thick lines at the tops of trees. It's a good idea when painting the twigs to immediately dab their ends with a tissue to lighten their value to replicate nature where the light catches them.

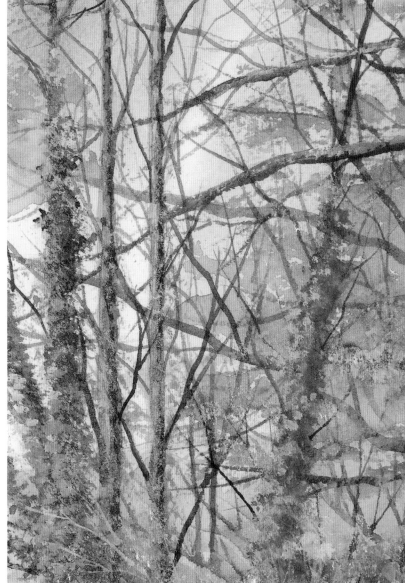

COUNTRY LANE – CLOSE UP

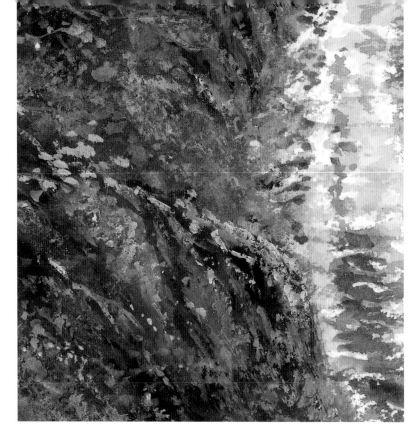

KEY POINTS

1 Paint a simple atmospheric sky as background.

2 Take care when painting the right-hand trees. Make sure that the branches and especially the twigs aren't painted too thick in form.

3 Use a damp sponge to stipple on the foliage. Try this on an off-cut of paper until you are satisfied that the paint is being deposited to your liking – not too dense and remember not to squeeze the sponge as you stipple.

4 Make sure the left-hand pine tree is a pleasing shape to balance the relatively leafless tree grouping on the right.

5 The track, although rutted, must appear light, to lead the viewer's eye into and out of the painting.

6 The banks are main features. Follow the stages described in the text – make them look real.

RIGHT-HAND BANK

Masking fluid was applied with a rigger brush to represent new growth. Leafy growth on the bank was replicated by stippling masking fluid on to the area with an old worn oil painter's brush. When dry the hedgerow and bank were painted. The masking was removed and a size 6 round brush used to paint soft green, yellows and sienna to represent rough texture.

LEFT-HAND BANK

This was to be painted in darker values, but I needed to indicate a few light-coloured leaves and rough texture here and there as would be apparent in reality. The best way to achieve this was to apply masking fluid by stippling with a worn oil painter's hog hair brush. When it was dry, various tones of Raw Sienna and Burnt Sienna were applied.

A Payne's Grey/Alizarin Crimson mix was used to create the darker values representing depth in the bank.

To illustrate the thin tree structures in the distance, I scratched them out with a cocktail stick. When the paint was completely dry the masking was removed with a putty eraser and soft greens, yellows and siennas were painted over the preserved white of the paper to represent the colours of the leaves and other vegetation. It is important that the bank is a darker tone than the opposite bank.

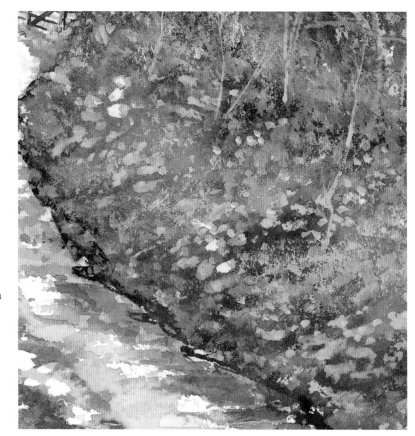

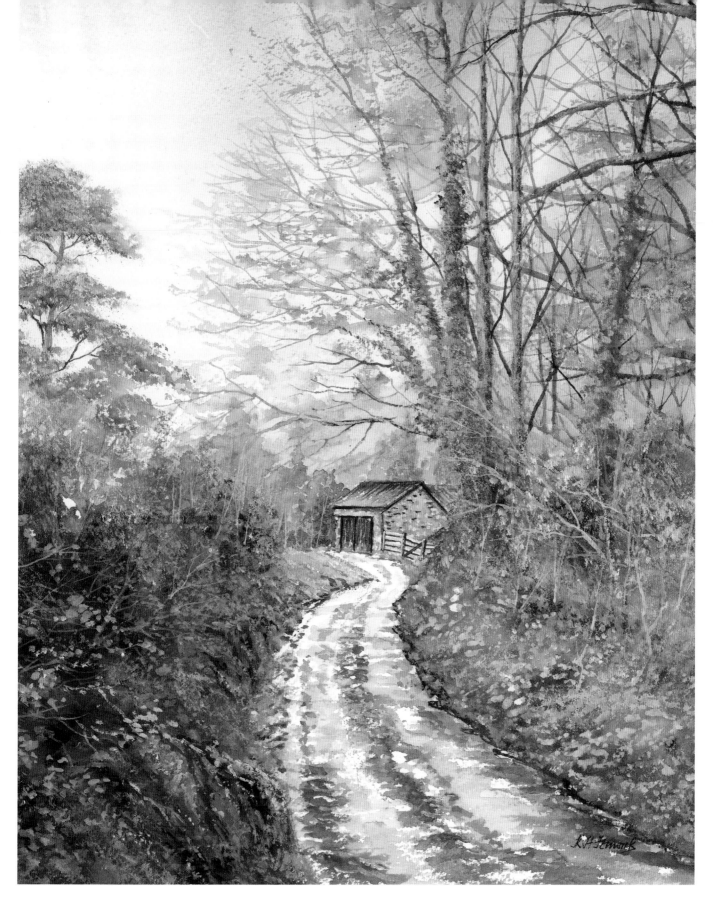

FINAL DETAILS

Using the rigger brush, the fence and gate at the side of the building were painted. A few light-coloured leaves were added using the rigger brush and the mixes already on the palette with a little white acrylic added to lighten the values. The edges of the track were given more definition using darker values.

My normal practice at this stage is to look at the painting over a few days and make any improvements that I feel are necessary.

COUNTRY LANE – CLOSE UP

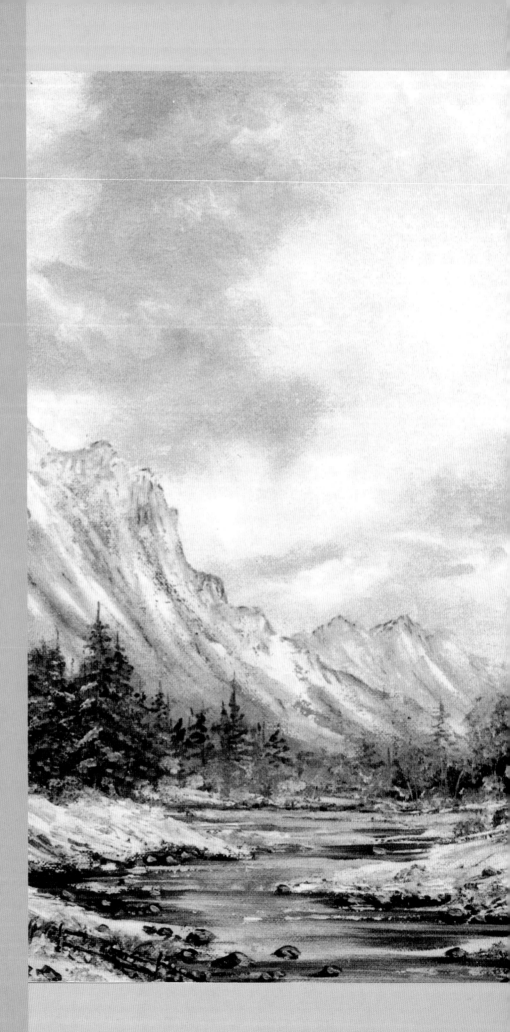

**Right: A Walk on the
Wild Side**

WINTER

Out of the bosom of the air

Out of the cloud–folds of her garments shaken,

Over the woodlands brown and bare,

Over the harvest–fields forsaken,

Silent and soft, and slow

Descends the snow.

Henry Wadsworth Longfellow

Winter is one of my favourite times of the year to paint. The fields are ploughed ready for the next generation of seeds, offering a surface full of subtle colour and interest. The trees are bare, presenting skeletal forms, except for evergreens such as conifers which often have an architectural beauty against a stark landscape.

There's nothing more beautiful than a snow-covered landscape on a crisp sunny day, and it provides the artist with a whole new world of inspiring compositions to paint. A partially frozen lake, frost and snow on winter trees and snow-capped mountains all present fresh challenges and a chance to put new techniques into practice.

MOUNTAIN VIEW – CLOSE UP

This scene was one of two 40-minute sketches, demonstrated to an art society. It is an imaginary landscape made up from a number of elements filed away in my memory and recalled like a jigsaw to create this composition.

As always, the tonal study is the starting point and the plan for the sketch. To emphasize the snow-capped peaks, a dramatic sky was required.

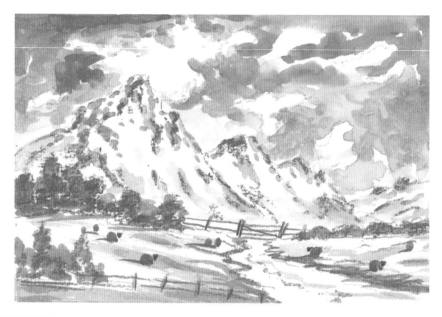

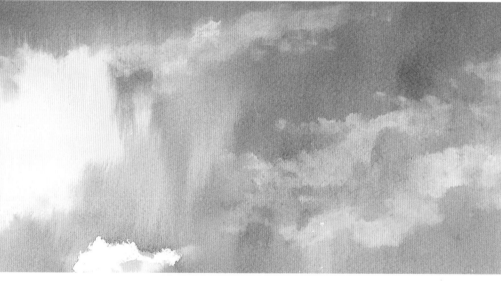

SKY

For speed and resulting freshness the 38 mm/1½ in hake brush is ideal, having the facility to hold large washes and then apply them quickly. By dabbing, brushing and twisting the brush in different directions, atmospheric skies like this one can be simply and speedily painted.

The hake was used to apply a pale Raw Sienna wash, followed by stiffer mixes of Payne's Grey, Cerulean Blue and Alizarin Crimson. Areas of Raw Sienna were left untouched and finally an absorbent tissue was used to remove paint to create the cloud structures. The paper was almost vertical, encouraging the paint to run, creating interesting sky features. The sky was dried using a hair-dryer. It was painted in less than four minutes, using the minimum of brush strokes.

WHAT YOU WILL NEED

PAPER:
Winsor & Newton 640 gsm/300 lb Rough

COLOURS:
Payne's Grey, Cerulean Blue, Alizarin Crimson, Raw Sienna, Burnt Sienna, Sap Green

BRUSHES:
Winsor & Newton Sceptre Gold II Series size 14 round, size 6 round, size 3 rigger, 19 mm/¾ in flat, 38 mm/1½ in hake

SUPPORTIVE:
White acrylic or gouache paint, palette knife, tissues

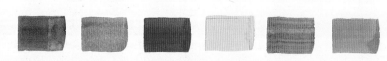

WINTER

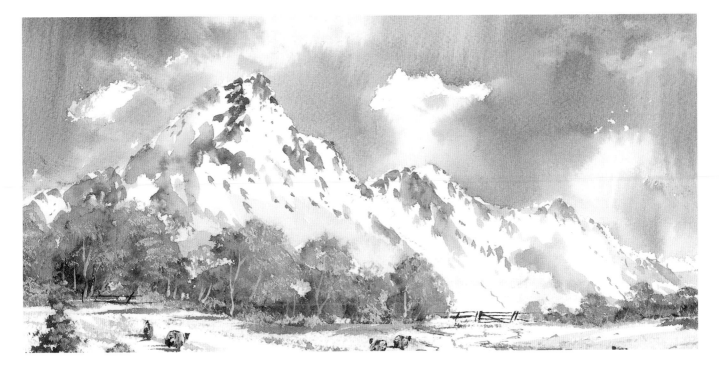

MOUNTAINS

The sky was painted working around the profile of the mountains. An occasional dab with a tissue ensured the paint didn't run into the mountain areas. The size 14 round brush was used to shape the mountains by working downwards from the peaks, applying paint with the point of the brush and then spreading it with quick flicks, using the side of the brush. A few quick dabs to deposit paint, followed by a few flicks to spread it and a few small dots of paint here and there, and the mountains are completed. Finally a little pale Raw Sienna was brushed upwards from the base of the mountains. A Payne's Grey/Cerulean Blue mix was used to paint the promontories projecting through the snow.

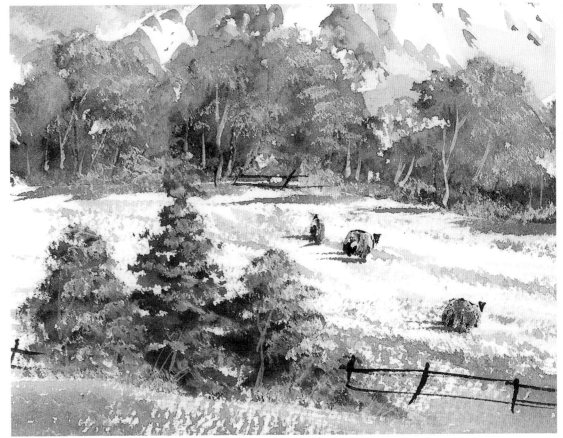

TREES AND BUSHES

The distant trees were painted using downward strokes with the side of the size 14 round brush. Mixes of Payne's Grey/Cerulean Blue/Burnt Sienna were used. Some of the tree structures were scratched in with a palette knife. A 19 mm/¾ in flat brush was used to paint the foreground trees, using the above mix with some Sap Green being added.

MOUNTAIN VIEW – CLOSE UP

KEY POINTS

1 Paint the sky wet-in-wet.

2 Dab and twist the hake brush to create the atmospheric sky.

3 Use absorbent tissues to remove paint.

4 Use a palette knife to scratch out tree structures.

5 Don't make the fencing square and regular.

6 Transfer the sky colours to the foreground to maintain colour harmony.

7 Add some sheep to add life and improve the composition.

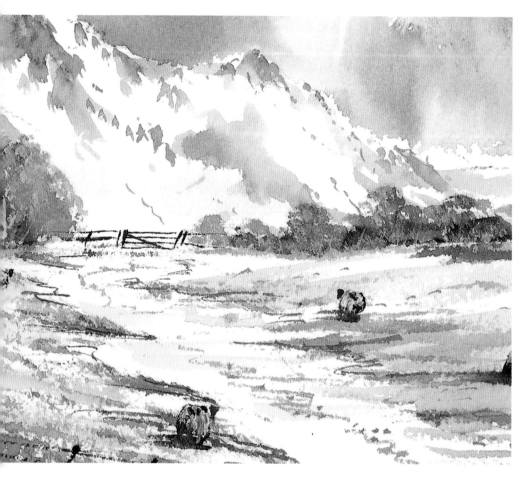

FOREGROUND

The edge of the hake brush was used to shape the path and add texture to the foreground. A Payne's Grey/Alizarin Crimson mix was used, followed by a hint of Raw Sienna to add warmth to the snow.

FENCE AND SHEEP

Fences are simply painted using the rigger brush. It is important that the spacing between the posts is approximately twice the height of the fence – square fences are not realistic. Keep them a simple two- or three-bar and don't make the fence posts perfectly vertical; by varying the angles, you will find they look better.

To paint sheep, simply paint horseshoes – extend the horseshoe to the left or right to make the body larger and add a triangle for the head. Follow the stages shown.

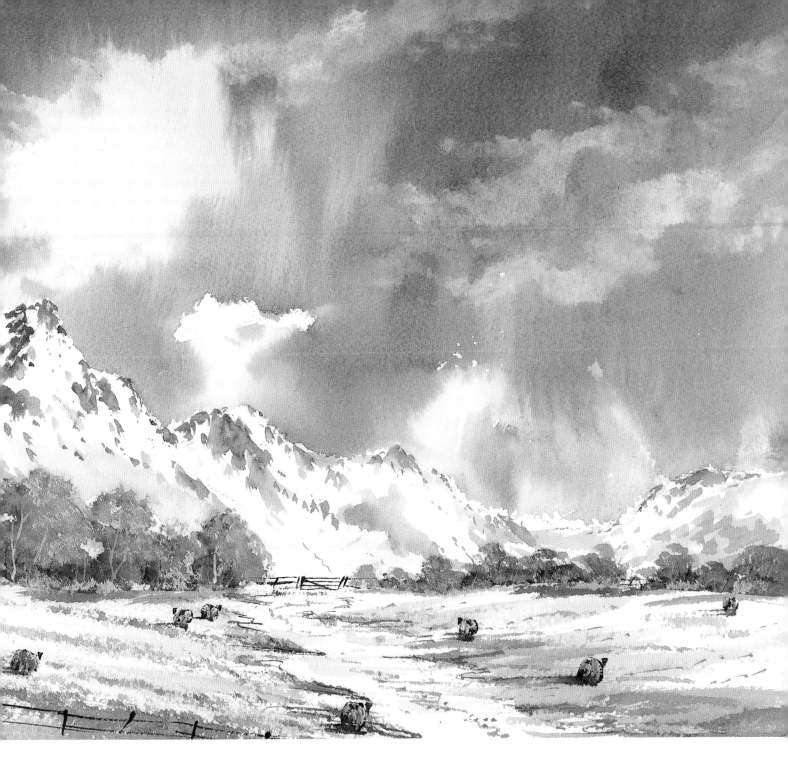

How to Paint Sheep

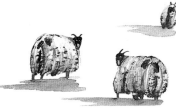

Stage 1

Paint horseshoe shapes to make the body of the sheep, larger horseshoes in the foreground and smaller ones in the distance, using a Payne's Grey/Burnt Umber mix.

Stage 2

If the sheep is looking to the right, add another horseshoe to the right and a triangle for the head; if it is looking to the left, add a horseshoe to the left and a triangle for the head.

Stage 3

When the paint is dry, add the white paint and give it a farmer's mark. Legs are optional depending on the conditions – if the sheep is standing in snow or long grass the legs will obviously not be visible. Paint shadows beneath the animal and add horns if needed.

MOUNTAIN VIEW – CLOSE UP

HEADING FOR A FALL – CLOSE UP

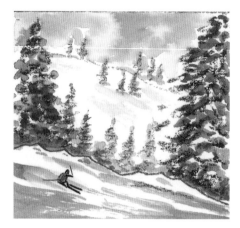

I have included this landscape as a simple exercise for you to complete. The secret here is the establishment of correct value patterns. The background must appear cold and misty, with the large trees in contrast.

I don't normally like to paint trees on both sides of a composition, but in this case I think it works. I produced several value patterns but prefer this one. I'm sure you will enjoy painting this landscape.

OUTLINE DRAWING

Very little drawing was done. The horizon was established, as was the foreground, and the distant tree position was indicated by simply placing a dot with the dark brown water-soluble crayon. A rough outline of the larger trees was drawn.

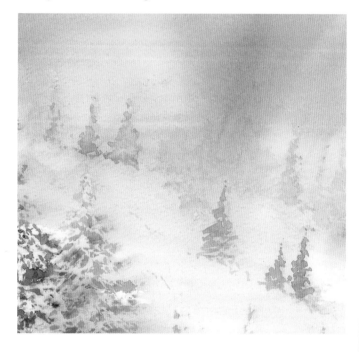

MASKING

A piece of tissue was crumpled almost to a point for control and then dipped into masking fluid. The larger trees were masked to create the effects of heavy snow on the foliage. To achieve this effect, I stippled with the tissue and flicked it downwards at the end of each stipple to create a ragged look.

SKY

A piece of 25 mm/1 in masking was positioned across the horizon line and using the hake brush loaded with a weak Payne's Grey/Alizarin Crimson mix, the sky was painted. I applied a few quick downward strokes of the hake to create the misty background.

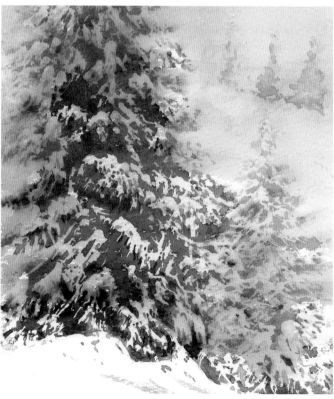

DISTANT TREES

When the paint was dry, the masking tape was carefully removed. The distant trees were painted using the corner of the 19 mm/¾ in flat brush loaded with a weak Payne's Grey.

MIDDLE-DISTANCE TREES

To create the effect of uneven, drifted snow at the base of the trees, a piece of masking tape was positioned across the paper. A mix of Payne's Grey/Cerulean Blue was used. The smaller trees in the centre were painted in a middle value. When that was dry, the two specimen trees were painted using darker values with a Payne's Grey/Cerulean Blue/Sap Green mix. The 19 mm/¾ in flat brush was used to paint the trees. When the paint was dry the masking tape and the masking fluid were removed, resulting in the effect of snow-laden trees.

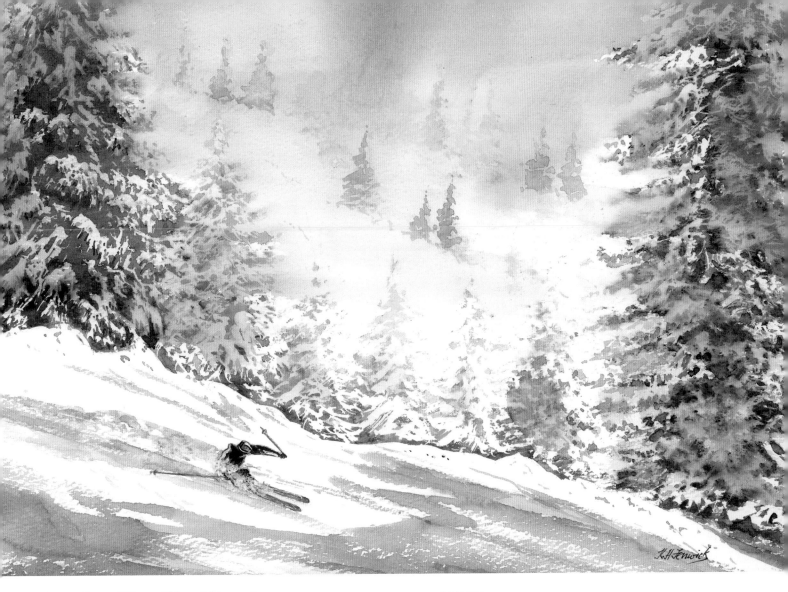

WHAT YOU WILL NEED

PAPER:
Winsor & Newton 300 gsm/140 lb Rough

BRUSHES:
Winsor & Newton Sceptre Gold II Series
size 14 round, 19 mm/¾ in flat, size 3 rigger,
38 mm/1½ in hake

COLOURS:
Payne's Grey, Cerulean Blue, Alizarin Crimson,
Sap Green

SUPPORTIVE:
Masking fluid, 25 mm/1 in masking tape, dark
brown water-soluble crayon, tissue

FOREGROUND AND SKIER

The side of a size 14 round brush was used to create some shadows on the foreground snow, using Payne's Grey. Finally, the skier was painted with the rigger brush. Don't risk spoiling your painting at this stage – practise painting the figure first on an off-cut of watercolour paper as the size and shape of the skier are important.

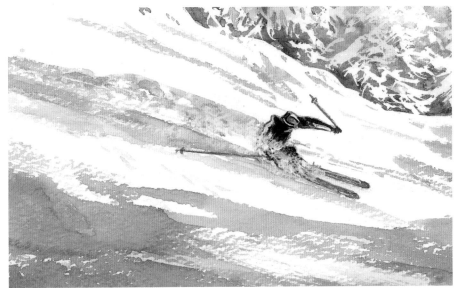

WOODLAND WALK – PROJECT

This area of woodland not far from my home is popular with walkers and picturesque at all times of the year.

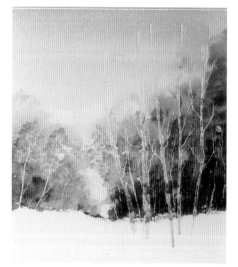

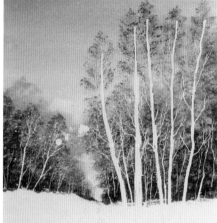

STAGE 3:
REMOVING MASKING
A putty eraser is ideal for removing masking fluid. It seems to bond with the masking and it is also gentle on the paper.

STAGE 4:
ADDING DETAIL
The texture on the trunks was painted by applying a Raw Sienna wash and when it was approximately one-third dry, brushing in Burnt Sienna, followed by Payne's Grey for the shadows.

STAGE 1:
BACKGROUND
Masking fluid was applied to the tree structures. Using the hake brush, a soft Cobalt Blue wash for the sky was followed by washes of Raw Sienna, Burnt Sienna, Sap Green and Cobalt Blue for the background foliage.

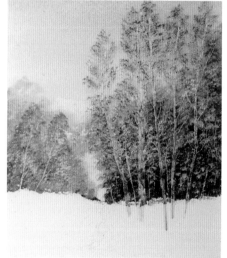

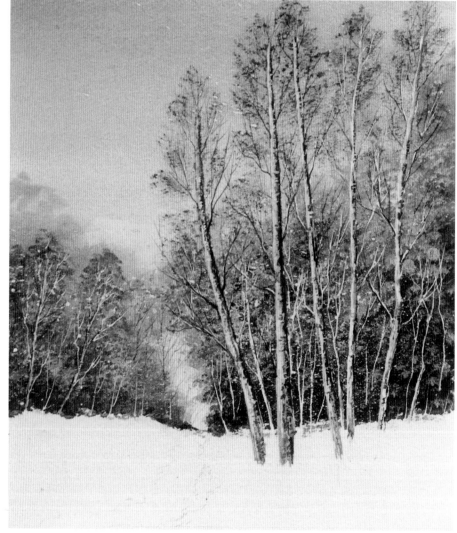

STAGE 2:
FOLIAGE
Using the same colours but stiffer paint, more detailed impressions of foliage were stippled using an old hog hair brush.

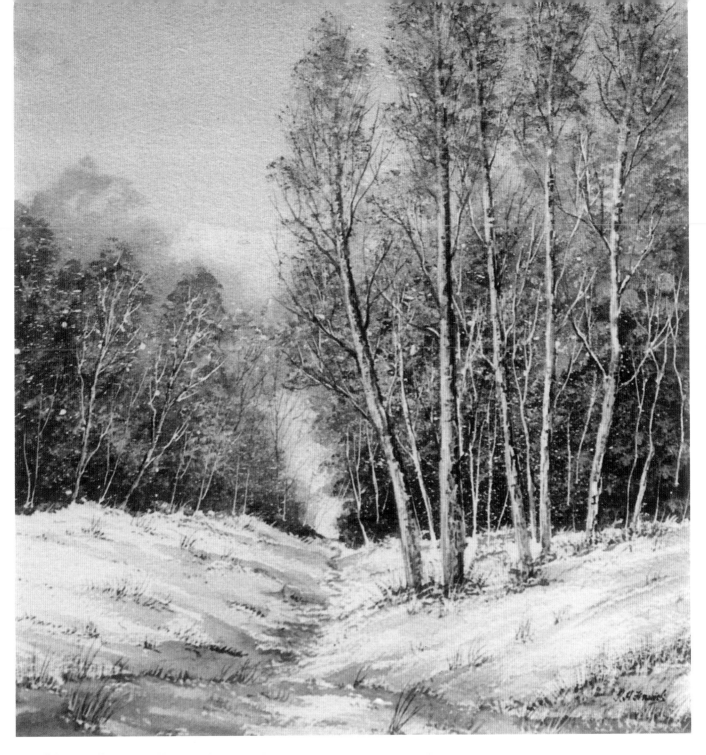

WHAT YOU WILL NEED

PAPER:
Winsor & Newton 640 gsm/300 lb Rough

BRUSHES:
Winsor & Newton Sceptre Gold II Series size 3 rigger, size 14 round, 38 mm/1½ in hake, hog hair

COLOURS:
Cobalt Blue, Raw Sienna, Burnt Sienna, Sap Green

SUPPORTIVE:
Masking fluid

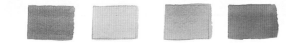

FINAL STAGE:
FOREGROUND
Using the side of the size 14 round brush, a Cobalt Blue/Alizarin Crimson mix was applied, working outwards from the path to represent shadows over the snow. Similarly, splashes of Raw Sienna were applied to harmonize the painting. Tufts of grass were painted with the rigger brush.

WOODLAND WALK – PROJECT

WILDERNESS – PROJECT

Painting a challenging foreground is possibly the most difficult task for the less experienced artist. The result is usually a few simple washes, displaying little texture and contributing almost nothing to the success of the painting. This is a landscape created entirely from my imagination, collated from a range of features encountered on my travels. It is a good example, allowing me to demonstrate my approach to painting a challenging foreground.

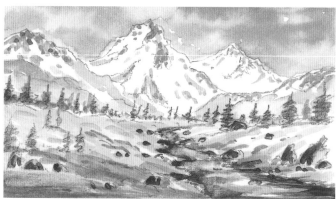

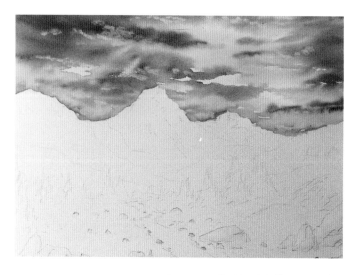

WHAT YOU WILL NEED

PAPER:
Saunders Waterford 640 gsm/300 lb Rough

BRUSHES:
Winsor & Newton Sceptre Gold II Series size 14 round, size 6 round, 19 mm/¾ in flat, 38 mm/1½ in hake, 13 mm/½ in round hog hair brush

COLOURS:
Payne's Grey, Cobalt Blue, Alizarin Crimson, Raw Sienna, Burnt Sienna, Sap Green

SUPPORTIVE:
Masking fluid, dark brown water-soluble crayon

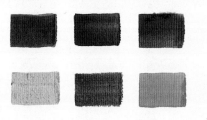

STAGE 1:

DRAWING, MASKING, SKY

The basic outline was drawn using a dark brown water-soluble crayon. Masking fluid was applied to the foreground rocks and those in the mountain stream.

Although there is plenty of detail in the foreground, I wanted to paint a warm sky, enabling me to transfer these sky colours into the foreground.

The sky was painted using the techniques you are now familiar with. Washes of Raw Sienna were applied in the centre, surrounded by washes of Cobalt Blue, the two colours blending together, and a mix of Cobalt Blue/Alizarin Crimson was used for the cloud formations.

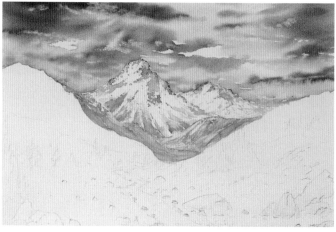

STAGE 2:

SNOW-CAPPED MOUNTAINS

These need to be sensitively painted. Using the size 14 round brush loaded with a Cobalt Blue/Alizarin Crimson mix, I painted the main shadows/promontories, taking care to leave lots of white paper uncovered. When the paint was about one-third dry, details were added using the rigger brush. It is important to pause and stand back after each layer of paint to determine where further paint needs to be laid in.

STAGE 3:
RIGHT MIDDLE DISTANCE

Following the structure of the mountain, sweeping strokes with the hake brush were made, beginning with a Raw Sienna wash followed by Sap Green to selected areas. Using the flat brush, a Payne's Grey/Alizarin Crimson mix was applied to the areas where the rocks were located. When this area was approximately one-third dry, I used the palette knife to move paint to create the rock formation.

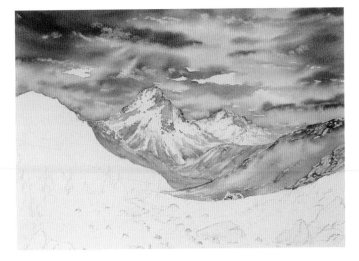

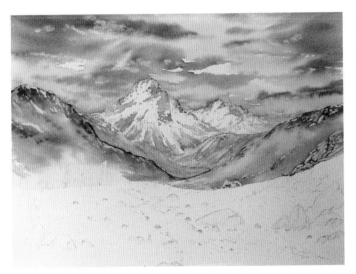

STAGE 4:
LEFT MIDDLE DISTANCE

Following the process described above, I completed the left-hand mountain. Note that this was painted as higher and a different shape to the mountain on the right.

When you are painting a real mountain range, it is important to select a viewpoint where the mountains display differing profiles and heights as this helps to create more interest in the painting.

STAGE 5:
FOREGROUND WASHES AND TREES

Apply several pale washes for the underpainting of the foreground. On the left foreground, Raw Sienna was covered by Sap Green and allowed to dry. The right foreground was Raw Sienna covered with a Payne's Grey/Burnt Sienna mix and allowed to dry.

The distant trees were painted small and in paler tones than those on the right bank to create a sense of distance, which is so important in this painting.

The trees and their shadows were painted using the flat brush loaded with mixes of Sap Green and Cobalt Blue. Note that the masking on the rocks has repelled the paint.

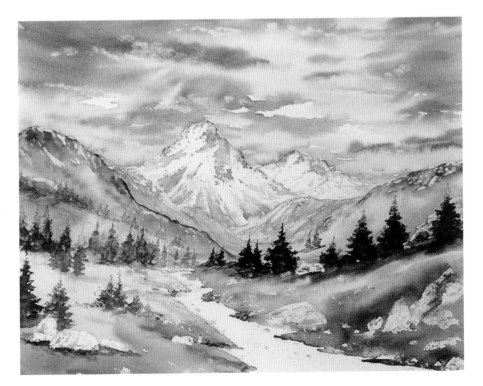

WILDERNESS – PROJECT

STAGE 6:
APPLYING DARKER VALUES

Using the side of the size 14 round brush, darker tones of Payne's Grey/Alizarin Crimson were put in to create depth in the foreground. Note that light areas were left uncovered between brush strokes.

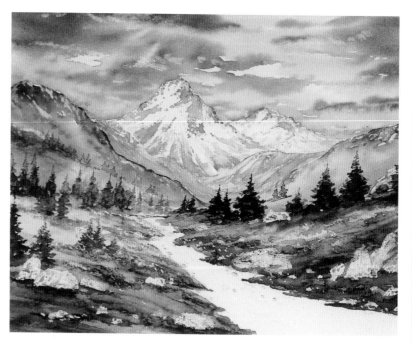

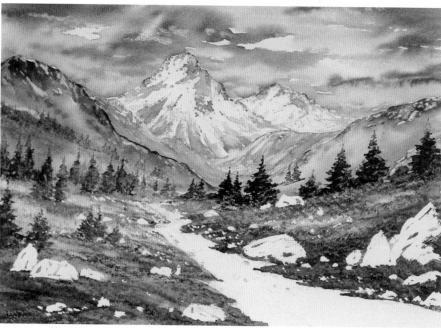

STAGE 7:
CREATING TEXTURE

The aim here is to create the effect of heather and low-growing vegetation to represent rough moorland. The most effective technique to achieve this is to stipple paint with an oil painter's hog hair brush. To simulate heather, I have used an Alizarin Crimson/Cobalt Blue mix, following on while still wet with a little white acrylic paint added to the mixture to produce highlights. The same approach was employed to paint rough vegetation, using Raw Sienna/Sap Green mixes with a little white acrylic paint added.

When the paint was completely dry, the masking was removed from all the rocks except those in the mountain stream.

KEY POINTS

1 Paint a warm, atmospheric sky using the techniques described in the text.

2 Take care not to overdo it when painting snow-capped mountains – remember, less is more.

3 Paint the trees in different sizes and values – and don't forget the need for recession.

4 Build up the foreground in stages – follow the techniques described in the text.

5 Paint the rocks using the wet-in-wet technique.

WINTER

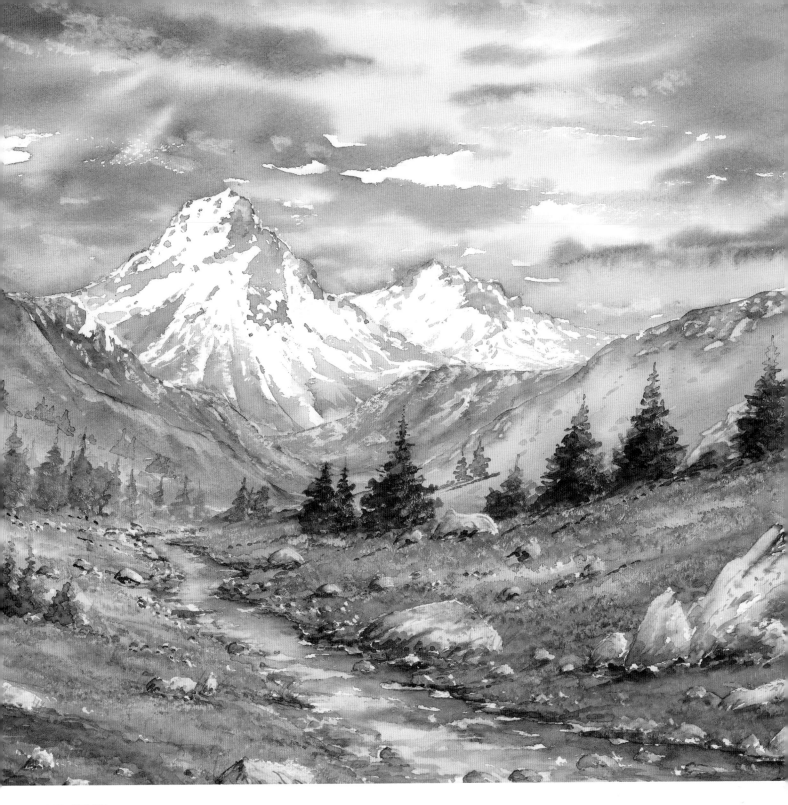

FINAL STAGE:
ROCKS, WATER, GLAZING

My intention here was to transfer some sky colour over to the foreground. Using light touches with the side of a soft size 14 round brush, sky colours were glazed over the foreground. This harmonized the painting, producing a warm glow.

The water was painted using the hake brush, the shadows being indicated with a Payne's Grey/Alizarin Crimson mix. It was important to leave expanses of paper uncovered. When the painting was dry, a little Raw Sienna was added to selected areas.

The masking was removed from the rocks in the mountain stream, then the rocks were painted a few at a time by applying an initial pale Raw Sienna wash and, when this was approximately one-third dry, brushing in a mix of Burnt Sienna and Payne's Grey/Burnt Sienna. The paint blended together wet-in-wet. A size 6 round brush was used to move the paint around to create the required effect.

Finally, the profile of the mountain on the left was softened by washing out a little of the colour.

THE WAY FORWARD

If you have systematically worked through this book and practised all the techniques and projects, you should be able to paint most elements in the landscape with confidence by now.

Don't attempt to copy the landscapes exactly – change colours, incorporate additional features and make them your own. Remember that practice makes perfect. Painting isn't a gift; it's more perspiration than inspiration. As your confidence grows, you will find that your failures become fewer and if something ambitious doesn't quite work out, you can remove paint (just wet the area and remove the paint with a tissue) then repaint that element to your satisfaction.

So what is the next stage? By joining one or more art societies you will have the opportunity to make friends with like-minded people. All art societies hold at least one exhibition annually and some exhibit much more frequently, giving you the opportunity to show your work and maybe earn a little money through sales to cover the cost of your materials. Most societies provide a list of visiting demonstrators, enabling you to observe how other artists approach their paintings, and if you're fortunate you may be able to learn from a professional artist.

When I first began painting there were no teaching videos available and few art and craft shows, so I was unable to see other artists at work. Today there are many videos available for purchase, enabling you to sit in the comfort of your home and watch artists with a range of styles demonstrate how they paint. I have made 20 such videos myself.

There are now numerous major art exhibitions worldwide, and visiting some of these will give you the chance to talk to professional artists, see them demonstrate techniques and obtain practical advice from them. Eventually you will develop your own style of painting that can be recognized as your handwriting in paint.

As your confidence grows, you will be able to exhibit your paintings with other artists. The experience of seeing your work exhibited and selling your first painting is hugely satisfying and exciting, and it tells you that all the effort and expense you have put in was worth it.

Eventually, if you are ambitious, you will want to hold your own solo exhibition. You will find that most professional artists began by exhibiting in their local library or in the waiting room at their doctor's surgery, or the foyer of a theatre or sports centre; any venue at all where their work could be seen by the public. Your next problem will be acquiring display boards. Local authorities often have stocks of these that can be hired, as do local schools, colleges and art societies. Don't be afraid to approach them and ask if they can oblige. Alternatively, your local library will have held exhibitions on the premises and should be able to advise you on sources for hiring display boards if they don't have their own available. You will also need publicity posters, which can be cheaply reproduced on a photocopier.

If your progress results in your ability to produce really good paintings you may wish to approach a recognized art shop with gallery attached or even a major gallery in your area. They will want to see examples of your work and may insist that you exhibit with other artists to begin with. Don't forget to enquire about your contribution towards costs. Such galleries require a percentage of the selling price of the painting and may also want a contribution towards mail shots and advertising, so take care that you are not caught out by unexpected fees.

If you like the idea of selling your paintings online, a quick search will produce many websites with this facility. Many galleries these days have an online presence and stands at art fairs rather than high street premises, so you can be sure that exhibiting online does work.

Visit every art show you can and read as many art books as possible – you will learn something from all of them. Use your initiative and don't let opportunities pass you by. Above all else – enjoy your painting. Good luck on your exciting journey!

Best wishes,

KEITH FENWICK

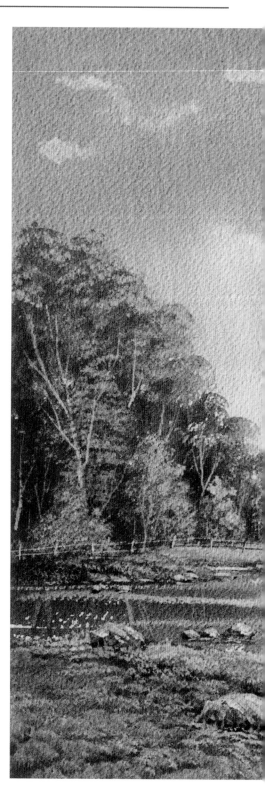

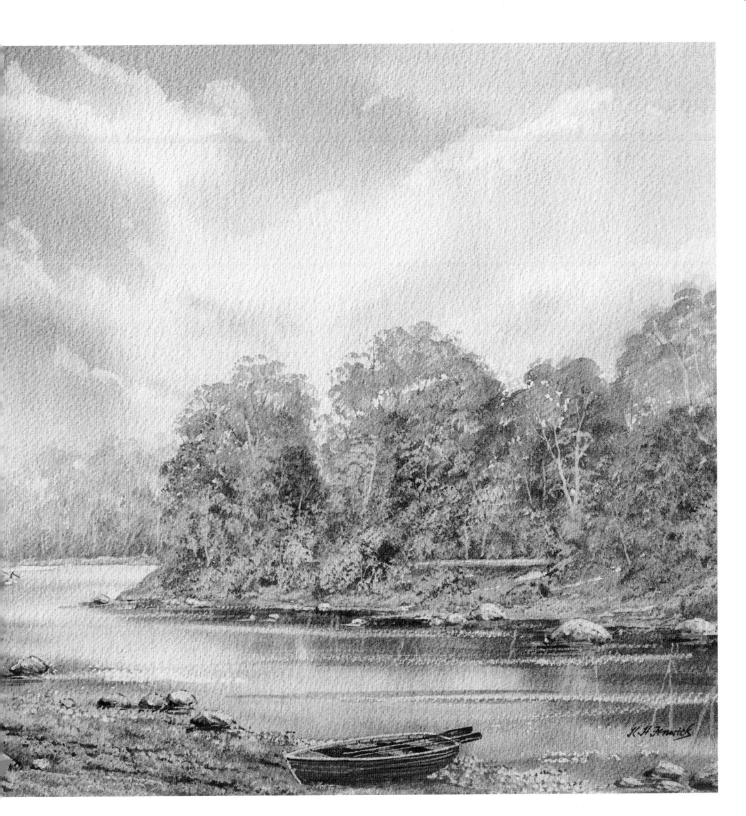

Above: Autumn Gold

PORTRAIT OF THE ARTIST

Keith Fenwick is one of the UK's leading teachers in painting techniques. He enjoys a tremendous following among leisure painters, who flock to his demonstrations and workshops at major fine art and craft shows.

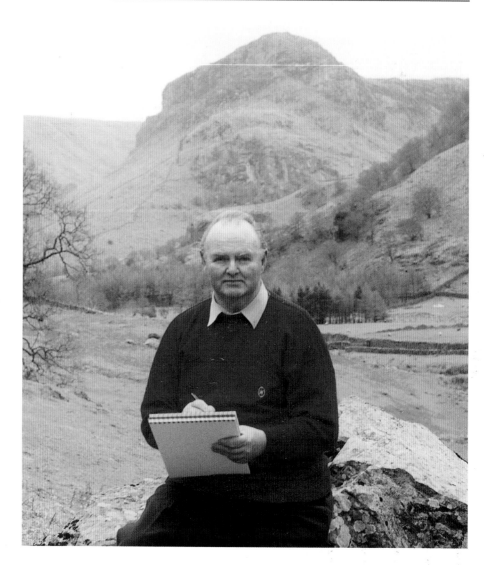

A chartered engineer, Keith holds several professional qualifications, including an honours degree. He served an engineering apprenticeship, becoming chief draughtsman before progressing to senior management.

After spending numerous years in management in both industry and further education, Keith took early retirement from his position as Associate Principal/Director of Sites and Publicity at one of the UK's largest colleges of further education in order to devote more time to his great love, landscape painting.

He now runs painting holidays in the UK and elsewhere in Europe and gives seminars and workshops nationwide. He demonstrates painting techniques to audiences at most major fine art and craft shows throughout the UK, and to the members of up to 50 art societies each year. He is also a principal demonstrator for Winsor & Newton. His expertise in landscape painting and experience in teaching, video-making and broadcasting ensure an understanding of student needs.

Keith has appeared on BBC and cable TV and presented Granada TV's *Art School*. He is a fellow of the Royal Society of Arts and a member of the Advisory Panel of the Society for All Artists. His paintings are in collections in the UK and other European countries, as well as in the USA, Canada, New Zealand, Australia, Japan and the Middle East.

Keith finds great personal satisfaction in encouraging those who have always wanted to paint but lack the confidence to try, as well as helping more experienced painters to develop their skills further. His books have all proved very popular, as have his 20 best-selling art teaching videos, which have benefited students worldwide. He is also a regular contributor to several art and craft magazines. He hopes that this book will be a constant companion to those wishing to improve their skills and experiment with new ways to paint the landscape.

Keith's previous books are:
Trees, Rocks and Running Water
Skies, Mountains and Lakes
Buildings, Bridges and Walls
Atmosphere, Mood and Light.